How to Handle Cults - Contending for the Truth Against the Spirit of Permissiveness © Copyright 2024 ● Dr. Jim Taylor

• • • •

ALL SCRIPTURE QUOTES are from the King James Bible except those verses compared and then the source is identified.

Although several other authors have been quoted or mentioned in this book, this author does not share or endorse the various theological positions of everyone who is mentioned. Additionally, it can be reasonably assumed that those mentioned would not necessarily agree with every position or viewpoint mentioned herein. The mere citing or mention of others is NOT to be considered an endorsement of their beliefs.

How to Handle Cults
Contending for the Truth Against the Spirit of Permissiveness

Dedication

As the years have rolled by I have seen several good friends begin well. For a time they seemed to be very much in line with what I believed. They spoke like I did. They sang the same songs. They followed the same preachers. They held the same set of standards and convictions. But something happened and they both fell away. Two of the men most dear to my heart both made the same mistake. They *thought* they were mature enough, smart enough, and strong enough, to study the materials of false religion and be okay.

They began well but they didn't end well at all. The last I heard, one man is now a New Ager while the other went from pastor to atheist. You have to wonder if either one was genuinely saved but we have no way of knowing the heart.

So, in a strange twist of irony, I want to dedicate this book to Robbie and Chris. I doubt you will ever actually read this book but if you do, just know that I still pray for you and hope that someday you will see the truth.

Preface

Cults fascinate us.

That's one reason why there is very little challenge to filling the seats of a college class on the subject of cults. Any YouTube video on cults will get thousands of hits almost effortlessly.

We want to know what it is that makes them what they are. We want to know what makes them different. We want to know what makes them dangerous.

This book is certainly not the best-seller on the subject of dealing with the cults. Dr. Walter Martin's now famous book on the Kingdom of the Cults will not be replaced as the classic textbook on the subject. However, as I had studied and taught the subject for many years, I wanted to provide a slightly different approach to the subject.

I want to begin with a basic foundation of what makes a group a cult. Is it because they have different practices? Is it because they dress differently?

Or does the Bible give us a working definition? I believe it does.

It is one thing to be in error concerning our beliefs. Error can be damaging in a limited sense. It is quite another to believe heresy. This will not only cause harm. It will destroy.

I should also note that this book has a particular "Asian" slant since it was mainly written for college classes to students in South Korea. Thus, it deals with cults and world religions that are most common in Korea. That being said, all of these same cults and world religions are a worldwide problem as well. So, even if you do not live in Korea, this book can be a great help to you.

Table of Contents

Introduction

I t is estimated that there are over 5000 cults active in the United States alone. I believe that the number is too small because first of all, there are cults that are rarely counted as such. Secondly, it seems that new cults pop up almost every day.

The word cult means something different to different people. Thoughts of David Koresh, and the Branch Davidians come to mind. Or maybe you think of Jim Jones and the horrible massacre that happened in Jonestown. This is where we get the no common idiom, "He drank the Kool-Aid".

And who can forget Heaven's Gate in California? Those people believed that the aliens were coming and they committed suicide. I don't think there's any question that cults can be extremely dangerous.

When I was younger, it was common to see the followers of Sun Myung Moon, better known as the Moonies, or the followers of Harry Krishna. Growing up in the Washington DC area, it was just one of those things. If you went to the Capitol, they were there. If you went to the museums, they were there. If you went to the airport, they were there.

And let's not forget the connection of the word "cult" with visions of witch covens, satanic rituals, weird loner groups, or blood sacrifices.

Taking all of this into consideration, we have a very broad brush to paint for us what a cult is. But to be honest, the idea of what constitutes a cult is broader than any of these.

If you "Google" the top ten cults in the world, you can find numerous lists including everyone from the Manson family to the KKK.

Sadly, many of these cults have listed some very influential people for example:

- *Hare Krishna* - estimated 1 million members – among whom are some famous people such as the Beatles, Abba, and many other musicians.

- *Scientology* - an estimated 8 million have shown an interest – among whom are some famous stars such as Kirstie Alley, Tom Cruise, John Travolta, Demi Moore, and Charlie Manson!

- *Catholicism* - Most people don't realize it but the largest cult in the world is probably the Catholic Church and there are scores of famous Catholics! As of January 2022, there is an estimated 1.3 billion Catholics worldwide.

Many Bible colleges like to divide the issue into two areas:

- *World religions* - Religions such as Buddhism, Islam, or Hinduism where there is no pretense of following the Bible as a holy book. They are not pretending to be Christianity.

- *Cults* - Any religion that uses the Bible, although inappropriately, to teach their false views. Normally we would put Catholicism, Mormonism, Jehovah's Witnesses, etc. in this category. They pretend to be authentic forms of Christianity.

We have not actually defined what a cult is yet. We will get to that at the appropriate time. But I would like to add that cults are not a new phenomenon. They have been around since the Garden of Eden.

Genesis 3:1-7 Now the serpent was more subtil than any beast of the field which the LORD God had made. And he said unto the woman, Yea, hath God said, Ye shall not eat of every tree of the garden? 2 And the woman said unto the serpent, We may eat of the fruit of the trees of the garden: 3 But of the fruit of the tree which is in the midst of the garden, God hath said, Ye shall not eat of it, neither shall ye touch it, lest ye die. 4 And the serpent said unto the woman, Ye shall not surely die: 5 For God doth know that in the day ye eat thereof, then your eyes shall be opened, and ye shall be as gods, knowing good and evil. 6 And when the woman saw that the tree was good for food, and that it was pleasant to the eyes, and a tree to be desired to make one wise, she took of the fruit thereof, and did eat, and gave also unto her husband with her; and he did eat. 7 And the eyes of them both were opened, and they knew that they were naked; and they sewed fig leaves together, and made themselves aprons.

What were the methods that the serpent used to cause the fall of man? He promised them Godhood. He also promised them prosperity. But what he delivered is exactly the opposite. Instead of becoming like God, Adam, and Eve, and by extension, the rest of the human race, became more like the devil. And instead of prosperity, we became spiritual paupers.

The methods that cults employ are the same age-old methods that were used in the garden.

The *two greatest attractions* to cults deal with:

- A *false hope of Godhood* (deification of man)
- An *empty promise of prosperity* (health/wealth preaching)

What did the serpent do to make his way seem attractive? ***How did Satan orchestrate the fall of man?*** The story is familiar to us.

- He began by ***attacking the Word of God.*** ("hath God said?")

Naturally, this characteristic is still practiced by false religions today. You will never find a cult that interprets the word of God the way that God intended it to be interpreted. They always add to, take away from, or re-interpret the Scriptures to fit their pet theology.

- Then secondly, the serpent ***attacked the moral character of God*** Himself.

Genesis 3:5 *For God doth know that in the day ye eat thereof, then your eyes shall be opened, and ye shall be as gods, knowing good and evil.*

Satan proposed that God was trying to keep a corner on knowledge. He wanted Eve to think that God was seeking to withhold something that would be beneficial for Eve, something she would enjoy.

The truth is, that God has always had the good of mankind at heart. If God was trying to withhold anything, He was trying to withhold the destruction and horror associated with sin.

Have you ever wondered why Satan tempted Eve in the first place? Why did he want Adam and Eve to disobey God? And what is even worse, knowing that eating the fruit would bring death, why did Satan want Adam and Eve to die? What would he gain from it?

The motive for his plans is seen in his own confession:

Isaiah 14:12-14 *How art thou fallen from heaven, O Lucifer, son of the morning! how art thou cut down to the ground, which didst weaken the nations!* ***13*** *For thou hast said in thine heart, I will ascend into heaven, I will exalt my throne above the stars of God: I will sit also upon the mount of the congregation, in the sides of the north:* ***14*** *I will ascend above the heights of the clouds; I will be like the most High.*

Initially, Satan desired to have a throne above all of creation and to be like the Most High. He never presumed that he could be above God. And he never says anything of that kind. No, rather, he desired to "*sit **also** upon the mount of the congregation*" and to "*be **like** the most High*".

To sit upon a throne denotes power. Satan desired to have power equal to God.

To be like the Most High denotes worship. Satan desired to receive worship.

And again, we are faced with two of the same motives that cult leaders have for deceiving their followers as well. It is a power grab and a lust for worship.

When Satan became prideful, thinking he deserved worship, he was cast out of Heaven and was told his fate.

Isaiah 14:15 *Yet thou shalt be brought down to hell, to the sides of the pit.*

Again, we are not to assume that Satan believes he can somehow overthrow God. He knows that he can't.

The reaction of the demons in the gospels indicates that there is fear of Christ among the demons. They realize that there is coming a time of torment and they do not desire for this torment to begin any earlier than necessary.

> *Matthew 8:29 And, behold, they cried out, saying, What have we to do with thee, Jesus, thou Son of God? art thou come hither to torment us before the time?*

Satan knows his future. Not only has it been clearly explained to him (Isaiah 14:15), but he has had 6000 years to read and ponder the curses of the Bible itself.

> *Revelation 12:12 Therefore rejoice, ye heavens, and ye that dwell in them. Woe to the inhabiters of the earth and of the sea! for the devil is come down unto you, having great wrath, because he knoweth that he hath but a short time.*

Having this background information as a foundation, we have come to the point where we can better discern Satan's motives for the fall of man.

You see, Satan knows that man was created to worship the LORD in a relationship of intimate and exclusive fellowship. And knowing that man was created to worship, he has been in an all-out battle to be the object of his worship.

In short, the spiritual war is not about who will ultimately have the final victory. It is a battle for the affections of the one creature that God made for communion with himself.

Knowing that he is a defeated foe, the only recourse that Satan retains is to try to rob God of something that God desires - fellowship with man.

This is not an act of desperation, but an act of rebellion. It is an act of rebellion to attempt to receive worship that belongs to God alone.

So this is the ultimate reason Satan has been ensnaring the hearts and minds of mankind. He blinds the lost so that they will not receive the truth and thereby enter into communion with God.

2 Corinthians 4:4 In whom the god of this world hath blinded the minds of them which believe not, lest the light of the glorious gospel of Christ, who is the image of God, should shine unto them.

Satan lures the believer into sin, which breaks fellowship with God.

James 4:4 Ye adulterers and adulteresses, know ye not that the friendship of the world is enmity with God? whosoever therefore will be a friend of the world is the enemy of God.

1 John 2:15-17 Love not the world, neither the things that are in the world. If any man love the world, the love of the Father is not in him. 16 For all that is in the world, the lust of the flesh, and the lust of the eyes, and the pride of life, is not of the Father, but is of the world. 17 And the world passeth away, and the lust thereof: but he that doeth the will of God abideth for ever.

Satan is called "the god of this world".

2 Corinthians 4:4 In whom the god of this world hath blinded the minds of them which believe not, lest the light of the glorious gospel of Christ, who is the image of God, should shine unto them.

The Greek word for "world" is the word "eon" which carries the idea of a particular period of time. A good example of this can be found in Matthew 24:3.

Matthew 24:3 And as he sat upon the mount of Olives, the disciples came unto him privately, saying, Tell us, when shall these things be? and what shall be the sign of thy coming, and of the end of the world?

"God of this world" is a title that is religious in nature. He is behind all false religious systems.

Leviticus 17:7 And they shall no more offer their sacrifices unto devils, after whom they have gone a whoring. This shall be a statute for ever unto them throughout their generations.

Deuteronomy 32:17 They sacrificed unto devils, not to God; to gods whom they knew not, to new gods that came newly up, whom your fathers feared not.

1 Corinthians 10:19-20 What say I then? that the idol is any thing, or that which is offered in sacrifice to idols is any thing? 20 But I say, that the things which the Gentiles sacrifice, they sacrifice to devils, and not to God: and I would not that ye should have fellowship with devils.

We are living in a day when witchcraft, idolatry, and false religion are not just practiced, but considered to be "in vogue".

It does not matter to Satan who you worship, so long as it is not the true God. It may be a false religion, humanism, or even atheism because he owns them all.

1 John 5:19 And we know that we are of God, and the whole world lieth in wickedness.

Scripture warns that in the last days, men would turn to cults. It was concerning false teachers that Paul wrote in 2 Cor 11:3,13-15.

2 Corinthians 11:3 But I fear, lest by any means, as the serpent beguiled Eve through his subtilty, so your minds should be corrupted from the simplicity that is in Christ.

2 Corinthians 11:13-15 For such are false apostles, deceitful workers, transforming themselves into the apostles of Christ. 14 And no marvel; for Satan himself is transformed into an angel of light. 15 Therefore it is no great thing if his ministers also be transformed as the ministers of righteousness; whose end shall be according to their works.

They masquerade behind a facade of spirituality:

1 Timothy 4:1-3 Now the Spirit speaketh expressly, that in the latter times some shall depart from the faith, giving heed to seducing spirits, and doctrines of devils; 2 Speaking lies in hypocrisy; having their conscience seared with a hot iron; 3 Forbidding to marry, and commanding to abstain from meats, which God hath created to be received with thanksgiving of them which believe and know the truth.

There have always been a few who have claimed to be God, but we are living in a day when many are proclaiming godhood. Jesus declared that rampant religious deception would be the first sign preceding his Second Coming.

***Matthew 24:3-5** And as he sat upon the mount of Olives, the disciples came unto him privately, saying, Tell us, when shall these things be? and what shall be the sign of thy coming, and of the end of the world? 4 And Jesus answered and said unto them, Take heed that no man deceive you. 5 For many shall come in my name, saying, I am Christ; and shall deceive many.*

Probably every Christian is in error somewhere because we are finite and fallible. What is the saying? To err is human? We need to remember that.

But we also need to remember that error is not necessarily heresy. Even though errors are serious and should be addressed they do not upset the foundation truths of Christianity.

Every cult must attack truth. Any presentation of a lie is an attack upon the truth.

This may be done boldly and directly but usually, it is done subtly.

> **Galatians 3:1** *O foolish Galatians, who hath bewitched you, that ye should not obey the truth, before whose eyes Jesus Christ hath been evidently set forth, crucified among you?*

In many cases, cult leaders will take an "intellectual" approach.

> **Colossians 2:8** *Beware lest any man spoil you through philosophy and vain deceit, after the tradition of men, after the rudiments of the world, and not after Christ.*

> **Colossians 2:19-20** *And not holding the Head, from which all the body by joints and bands having nourishment ministered, and knit together, increaseth with the increase of God. **20** Wherefore if ye be dead with Christ from the rudiments of the world, why, as though living in the world, are ye subject to ordinances,*

They prey on those who have not been grounded in truth.

> **Romans 16:17-18** *Now I beseech you, brethren, mark them which cause divisions and offences contrary to the doctrine which ye have learned; and avoid them. **18** For they that are such serve not our Lord Jesus Christ, but their own belly; and by good words and fair speeches deceive the hearts of the simple.*

We must not forget that cults are ***very good at deception***.

2 Timothy 3:5 Having a form of godliness, but denying the power thereof: from such turn away.

From all outer appearances, they may have every characteristic of holy service. We cannot tell a difference in their form. And we must be careful when we discern according to their power. They do not have the power of God but that doesn't mean they are powerless.

This is why we must not base our judgment on outer appearance. And yet we must judge!

1 John 4:1 Beloved, believe not every spirit, but try the spirits whether they are of God: because many false prophets are gone out into the world.

John 7:24 Judge not according to the appearance, but judge righteous judgment.

Since error is serious, it must be confronted. And it does not matter what the source of that error may be. It may even be in someone that we know, love, and honor. An error must be confronted.

Galatians 2:11-14 But when Peter was come to Antioch, I withstood him to the face, because he was to be blamed. 12 For before that certain came from James, he did eat with the Gentiles: but when they were come, he withdrew and separated himself, fearing them which were of the circumcision. 13 And the other Jews dissembled likewise with him; insomuch that Barnabas also was carried away with their dissimulation. 14 But when I saw that they walked not uprightly according to the truth of the gospel, I said unto Peter before them all, If thou, being a Jew, livest after the manner of Gentiles, and not as do the Jews, why compellest thou the Gentiles to live as do the Jews?

On the other hand, some are not only in error but also pervert the Gospel. These are not to be confronted but exposed and expelled.

Galatians 1:7-9 Which is not another; but there be some that trouble you, and would pervert the gospel of Christ. 8 But though we, or an angel from heaven, preach any other gospel unto you than that which we have preached unto you, let him be accursed. 9 As we said before, so say I now again, If any man preach any other gospel unto you than that ye have received, let him be accursed.

How then are we to know the difference between who to confront and who to expel?

Certain symptoms will reveal this sickness. If you see the symptoms, watch for the sickness. If you see the sickness, operate!

Galatians 5:7-12 Ye did run well; who did hinder you that ye should not obey the truth? 8 This persuasion cometh not of him that calleth you. 9 A little leaven leaveneth the whole lump. 10 I have confidence in you through the Lord, that ye will be none otherwise minded: but he that troubleth you shall bear his judgment, whosoever he be. 11 And I, brethren, if I yet preach circumcision, why do I yet suffer persecution? then is the offence of the cross ceased. 12 I would they were even cut off which trouble you.

So what is a cult? Biblically, a cult may be defined as those that have added to, changed, or eliminated those things that are considered the fundamentals of Bible doctrine.

We are not to think that other denominations are cults. They may be in error concerning one thing or another, but if their error does not lead a person to hell, they may be wrong, but they are not a cult.

Walter Martin, in *The Kingdom of the Cults*, defined a cult as "any religious group which differs significantly in some one or more respects as to belief or practice, from those religious groups which are regarded as the normative expressions of religion in our total culture."

Due to various definitions by good people, we should be careful how we use the term. It should be clearly defined by the user. Bible terms describing error are much more helpful:

- "false prophets" (Mt. 7:15; 24:24)
- "heresies" (2 Pet. 2:1)
- "heretic" (Tit. 3:10)
- "false teacher" (2 Pet. 2:1)
- "false apostles, deceitful workers" (2 Co. 11:13)
- "doctrines of devils" (1 Tim. 4:1)
- "tradition of men" (Col. 2:8)
- "evil workers" (Ph. 3:2)
- "another gospel" (2 Cor. 11:4; Gal. 1:6)
- "antichrists" (1 Jn. 3:18)
- "evil men and seducers" (2 Tim. 3:13)
- "deceivers" (2 Tim. 3:13)
- "every wind of doctrine" (Eph. 4:14)

Again, we should be careful how we use the term. A cult is any movement, philosophy, group, church, or denomination that does not stand biblically in the following:

- ***The doctrine of Bibliology*** - that the Bible is the rule of faith and is complete. That no other so-called "holy book" exists or is required.

- ***The doctrine of Christ*** - in His deity or humanity, in His vicarious atonement; in his Lordship over His creation.

- ***The doctrine of salvation*** - in that man is saved by grace through faith without any blessing, benefit, or necessity of works.

Here is a definition from the Bible which sums up what is a cult:

2 Peter 2:1 *But there were false prophets also among the people, even as there shall be false teachers among you, who privily shall bring in damnable heresies, even denying the Lord that bought them, and bring upon themselves swift destruction.*

"Heresy" is an important word to define. The word heresy is a transliteration of the Greek word "αἱρεσις" (hairesis) which basically means a school or sect of a particular doctrine.

Acts 5:17 Then the high priest rose up, and all they that were with him, (which is the sect of the Sadducees,) and were filled with indignation,

Acts 15:5 But there rose up certain of the sect of the Pharisees which believed, saying, That it was needful to circumcise them, and to command them to keep the law of Moses.

One Greek scholar says it has the primary idea of choosing an opinion that is contrary to that which is normally received.

"Damnable" is another important word. This is the Greek word "ἀπώλεια" (apoleia) and is translated in various ways in the KJV:

• Perdition (2 Peter 3:7)

2 Peter 3:7 But the heavens and the earth, which are now, by the same word are kept in store, reserved unto fire against the day of judgment and perdition of ungodly men.

• Destruction (Matthew 7:13)

Matthew 7:13 Enter ye in at the strait gate: for wide is the gate, and broad is the way, that leadeth to destruction, and many there be which go in thereat:

• Waste (Matthew 26:8)

Matthew 26:8 But when his disciples saw it, they had indignation, saying, To what purpose is this waste?

• Damnation (2 Peter 2:3)

2 Peter 2:3 And through covetousness shall they with feigned words make merchandise of you: whose judgment now of a long time lingereth not, and their damnation slumbereth not.

The point is pretty clear. "Damnable" speaks of destruction but not merely physical, it especially speaks in a spiritual sense.

If the doctrinal position of any group places the mode of salvation in the hands of man, it qualifies as a cult. (Tit 3:5) There are several methods by which this is employed:

- By underrating the powers of Christ not only to save but also to intercede.

- By adding stipulations that man must perform before Calvary can be effectual.

- By assuming that Christ was not God in the flesh. (1 Tim 3:16; 2 Cor 5:19)

Thus, my definition of a cult is "***any teaching, if believed, that will cause you to be eternally lost***". By this definition Catholicism, Mormonism, Buddhism, and many others, are cults because they teach a different form of salvation other than the biblical viewpoint of salvation by grace.

We must never forget that there tends to be a tendency to demonize others who are different from us. We should also try to remember that there is a difference between error and heresy – believing that foot-washing is an ordinance of the church is an error but it is not heresy.

Many differ in the area of service but agree on the mode of salvation. Cults may agree with true Christianity in the area of service but *all cults differ upon the mode of salvation!* For example, The Church of Christ baptizes by immersion. ***But*** they view baptism as essential for salvation!

Depending on whose website you read, just about everyone has been accused of being a cult:

- Southern Baptists (https://www.reddit.com/r/atheism/comments/d44nwd/southern_baptists_are_a_cult/?rdt=52975)

- Independent Fundamentalists (http://www.baptistdeception.com/)

- Presbyterians (http://www.prime.org/Sewers.html)

- United Methodists (http://locustsandhoney.blogspot.com/2008/12/my-escape-from-cult-of-united-methodist.html)

- Christianity (http://freethought.mbdojo.com/cult_of_christianity.html)

- Independent Fundamental Baptists (https://cultstories.com/cults/denomination-a-sample-of-baptist-cults)

And the sad point is that everyone has their reason for believing someone else is a cult. So what should be the basis?

In keeping with our definition - "***any teaching, if believed, will cause you to be eternally lost***" – the doctrine of salvation becomes the measuring stick for identifying cults.

> ***Ephesians 2:8-9*** *For by grace are ye saved through faith; and that not of yourselves: it is the gift of God:* ***9*** *Not of works, lest any man should boast.*

> ***Titus 3:5*** *Not by works of righteousness which we have done, but according to his mercy he saved us, by the washing of regeneration, and renewing of the Holy Ghost;*

Therefore, any group that denies, adds to, or takes away from the work of Christ at Calvary is a cult.

Researchers who have taken a hard look at cults and cult leaders have identified certain characteristics, or, for this study, certain symptoms, that predominantly exist in a cult's social system.

There is usually a charismatic authority figure. The leaders seek to form an emotional bond with the followers. This practically guarantees that their actions would appear legitimate.

Cult leaders must maintain authority or they lose control of the group.

Jeremiah 5:31 The prophets prophesy falsely, and the priests bear rule by their means; and my people love to have it so: and what will ye do in the end thereof?

Many times this desire is expressed under the guise of "pastoral authority". While it is true that a pastor has authority, it is still Christ who is the head of the church.

Colossians 1:18 And he is the head of the body, the church: who is the beginning, the firstborn from the dead; that in all things he might have the preeminence.

Colossians 2:18-19 Let no man beguile you of your reward in a voluntary humility and worshipping of angels, intruding into those things which he hath not seen, vainly puffed up by his fleshly mind, 19 And not holding the Head, from which all the body by joints and bands having nourishment ministered, and knit together, increaseth with the increase of God.

The need for a cult leader to be the authority is sometimes seen in their rejection of other men of God.

3 John 1:9-10 I wrote unto the church: but Diotrephes, who loveth to have the preeminence among them, receiveth us not. 10 Wherefore, if I come, I will remember his deeds which he doeth, prating against us with malicious words: and not content therewith, neither doth he himself receive the brethren, and forbiddeth them that would, and casteth them out of the church.

The general purpose of charismatic authority is to provide leadership. The specific goal is for the leader to be accepted as the legitimate authority and to offer direction.

This is accomplished through privilege and command. The desired effect, of course, is that members will believe in and identify with the leader.

Then, ***there is typically some form of a control system***. This is the system of rules which guide the operation of the group as well as rules and regulations which guide the individual.

The control system provides an organizational structure that incorporates both rewards and punishment with the desired effect of compliance and unquestioned obedience.

Typically, there will be ***some form of communal influence***. This is a social network that helps to mold or reinforce compliance through experiential influences.

The specific goal is to create institutionalized group norms and an established code of conduct by which members are expected to live. This is accomplished by various methods of peer and leadership pressure, and through social-psychological influence and modeling.

There will be a ***"new" or "unique" way of approaching the Scriptures***.

Cult leaders will invariably stray from using scripture. Their message is often unbiblical. They become ear ticklers.

> ***Jeremiah 5:12-13*** *They have belied the LORD, and said, It is not he; neither shall evil come upon us; neither shall we see sword nor famine:* ***13*** *And the prophets shall become wind, and the word is not in them: thus shall it be done unto them.*

> ***Jeremiah 6:14*** *They have healed also the hurt of the daughter of my people slightly, saying, Peace, peace; when there is no peace.*

Their message is empty and leads to ungodliness. The fruit of their teaching leads to a denial of the righteous standards of a holy God.

Jeremiah 23:14 I have seen also in the prophets of Jerusalem an horrible thing: they commit adultery, and walk in lies: they strengthen also the hands of evildoers, that none doth return from his wickedness: they are all of them unto me as Sodom, and the inhabitants thereof as Gomorrah.

2 Timothy 2:16-17 But shun profane and vain babblings: for they will increase unto more ungodliness. 17 And their word will eat as doth a canker: of whom is Hymenaeus and Philetus;

In every case, there is a departure from historical Christianity.

Jeremiah 6:16 Thus saith the LORD, Stand ye in the ways, and see, and ask for the old paths, where is the good way, and walk therein, and ye shall find rest for your souls. But they said, We will not walk therein.

2 Peter 2:15 Which have forsaken the right way, and are gone astray, following the way of Balaam the son of Bosor, who loved the wages of unrighteousness;

There is no new truth! If it's true, it is not new. If it is new, it is not true. There is often ***an attempt to replace truth with worldliness*** and this is a major doctrinal trend in the prosperity gospel preachers!

1 John 4:5-6 They are of the world: therefore speak they of the world, and the world heareth them. 6 We are of God: he that knoweth God heareth us; he that is not of God heareth not us. Hereby know we the spirit of truth, and the spirit of error.

Jude 1:16 These are murmurers, complainers, walking after their own lusts; and their mouth speaketh great swelling words, having men's persons in admiration because of advantage.

Great emphasis is placed on materialism.

Jeremiah 6:13 For from the least of them even unto the greatest of them every one is given to covetousness; and from the prophet even unto the priest every one dealeth falsely.

While proposing that you may prosper, they devour the widow. The motive behind their message is self-gain.

Luke 20:47 Which devour widows' houses, and for a shew make long prayers: the same shall receive greater damnation.

2 Peter 2:3 And through covetousness shall they with feigned words make merchandise of you: whose judgment now of a long time lingereth not, and their damnation slumbereth not.

2 Peter 2:14 Having eyes full of adultery, and that cannot cease from sin; beguiling unstable souls: an heart they have exercised with covetous practices; cursed children:

There is often an emphasis on outward appearance, equating it with spirituality.

Matthew 23:23 Woe unto you, scribes and Pharisees, hypocrites! for ye pay tithe of mint and anise and cummin, and have omitted the weightier matters of the law, judgment, mercy, and faith: these ought ye to have done, and not to leave the other undone.

This can be manifested in many ways:

- By placing undue attention on diet, dress, or recreation, while neglecting faith, hope, and love. (Gal 5:1-6)

- By equating riches with godliness.

- By manipulating the people to "give it all" because poverty is godly.

- By implying that we need not be concerned with the matter of holiness because we have liberty. (Gal 5:13)

These are the characteristics that are most often seen in cult groups. We can think of them as symptoms of the sickness. When you see these characteristics, it is time to look deeper. If we find that the symptoms lead to the sickness, it is time to operate.

The Sickness - Denial of the Doctrines of Christ

Every cult must deal with the person of Jesus Christ. He cannot be ignored. There is just too much evidence of His existence. There is just too much evidence of His power and ministry.

So rather than acknowledge Jesus as Lord and Saviour, God in the flesh, cults will pervert the doctrines of Christ.

One of the most basic denials is *a denial of Christ's deity*.

> *1 John 4:1-3 Beloved, believe not every spirit, but try the spirits whether they are of God: because many false prophets are gone out into the world. 2 Hereby know ye the Spirit of God: Every spirit that confesseth that Jesus Christ is come in the flesh is of God: 3 And every spirit that confesseth not that Jesus Christ is come in the flesh is not of God: and this is that spirit of antichrist, whereof ye have heard that it should come; and even now already is it in the world.*

> *2 John 1:7-9 For many deceivers are entered into the world, who confess not that Jesus Christ is come in the flesh. This is a deceiver and an antichrist. 8 Look to yourselves, that we lose not those things which we have wrought, but that we receive a full reward. 9 Whosoever transgresseth, and abideth not in the doctrine of Christ, hath not God. He that abideth in the doctrine of Christ, he hath both the Father and the Son.*

There are very few who deny that Jesus existed, but many deny his virgin birth or His deity. And why? Because an admission that Jesus is God is an admission that He is the authority and His teachings are supreme.

A second denial is a *denial of Christ's work of grace*.

> *Hebrews 13:9 Be not carried about with divers and strange doctrines. For it is a good thing that the heart be established with grace; not with meats, which have not profited them that have been occupied therein.*

Since every cult is a system of works, then salvation by grace must be denied!

To emphasize outward appearance, the principle doctrine of grace must be either perverted or altogether denied.

> *Galatians 3:1-3 O foolish Galatians, who hath bewitched you, that ye should not obey the truth, before whose eyes Jesus Christ hath been evidently set forth, crucified among you? 2 This only would I learn of you, Received ye the Spirit by the works of the law, or by the hearing of faith? 3 Are ye so foolish? having begun in the Spirit, are ye now made perfect by the flesh?*

Young believers who are concerned about "living right" are most often the target of this type of approach. Compare Galatians 1:6 with Galatians 1:11:

> *Galatians 1:6 I marvel that ye are so soon removed from him that called you into the grace of Christ unto another gospel:*

> *Galatians 1:11 But I certify you, brethren, that the gospel which was preached of me is not after man.*

The Galatian believers, though they were saved, were still deceived.

A third denial is the denial of the liberty and freedom that is given in Christ. And again, we see this in the Galatian believers as well.

> *Galatians 2:4 And that because of false brethren unawares brought in, who came in privily to spy out our liberty which we have in Christ Jesus, that they might bring us into bondage:*

Remember, Satan does not care what you focus your attention upon as long as it is not Christ.

Believe it or not, as long as you are focusing on your temptations and weaknesses, you will live in defeat. You may even overcome those weaknesses, but you will have still taken your eyes off Jesus. The only way to live victoriously is to die to self.

***Galatians* 2:20** *I am crucified with Christ: nevertheless I live; yet not I, but Christ liveth in me: and the life which I now live in the flesh I live by the faith of the Son of God, who loved me, and gave himself for me.*

***Galatians* 5:22-23** *But the fruit of the Spirit is love, joy, peace, longsuffering, gentleness, goodness, faith,* **23** *Meekness, temperance: against such there is no law.*

So, the symptoms may vary but the sickness itself is always the same - a denial of the doctrines of Christ.

Dealing With a Cult Organization

Now that we have identified some principles for identifying a cult, how do we deal with them?

As we have already noted, every cult must attack truth. Any presentation of a lie is an attack upon the truth. This may be done boldly and directly but usually, it is done subtly, often using an intellectual approach to prey on those who are not grounded in the truth.

Their mode of operation is always to deceive. As Christians, we are commanded to defend the truth.

Jude 1:3 Beloved, when I gave all diligence to write unto you of the common salvation, it was needful for me to write unto you, and exhort you that ye should earnestly contend for the faith which was once delivered unto the saints.

This was one of Paul's primary motives.

Ephesians 1:7 In whom we have redemption through his blood, the forgiveness of sins, according to the riches of his grace;

Ephesians 1:17 That the God of our Lord Jesus Christ, the Father of glory, may give unto you the spirit of wisdom and revelation in the knowledge of him:

Many of us have to deal with cult organizations and must make sound biblical decisions concerning how to react to them. Sometimes it is difficult to make the right decisions. For example:

A local mobster decided he would build a stripper's club outside of a military base in Virginia. At the time, something like this had never been done and the county did not have sufficient laws to prevent it. However, the good people of the community did not want it and so several organizations began to speak out against it. A Mormon leader approached several churches with the idea that they should band together and fight for their cause. However, the pastors responded that they should fight for the community but not together since they did not have the same doctrine. Their morality might have been the same, but they could not take the risk of having their doctrinal stance confused with that of the Mormons.

The guidelines of the Scriptures are very clear. We are not to offer cooperation or support on any issue. This is called ecclesiastic separation.

Romans 16:17-18 Now I beseech you, brethren, mark them which cause divisions and offences contrary to the doctrine which ye have learned; and avoid them. 18 For they that are such serve not our Lord Jesus Christ, but their own belly; and by good words and fair speeches deceive the hearts of the simple.

We must not compromise for the sake of "strength in numbers". A wise preacher once said, "Me and God make a majority!"

2 Timothy 4:16-18 At my first answer no man stood with me, but all men forsook me: I pray God that it may not be laid to their charge. 17 Notwithstanding the Lord stood with me, and strengthened me; that by me the preaching might be fully known, and that all the Gentiles might hear: and I was delivered out of the mouth of the lion. 18 And the Lord shall deliver me from every evil work, and will preserve me unto his heavenly kingdom: to whom be glory for ever and ever. Amen.

There *will* be times when it may be necessary to denounce a cult organization by name.

In my many years in the pastorate, I have seen waves of cult influence sweep through faith communities and some churches didn't stand up under the attacks. The pastors, in many cases, did not sufficiently warn the people.

However, when doing so, keep in mind that our motive must be for edification:

> ***Ephesians 4:29*** *Let no corrupt communication proceed out of your mouth, but that which is good to the use of edifying, that it may minister grace unto the hearers.*

Some would disagree with naming names but it is not only necessary but also biblical. How many times did Jesus warn the apostles concerning the Pharisees, Sadducees, and Herodians? If He only warned them once, it is enough to prove the point. Here is one example from Matthew:

> ***Matthew 16:6*** *Then Jesus said unto them, Take heed and beware of the leaven of the Pharisees and of the Sadducees.*

> ***Mark 8:15*** *And he charged them, saying, Take heed, beware of the leaven of the Pharisees, and of the leaven of Herod.*

On the other hand, avoid the "hobby-horse syndrome". This is when the main topic that we speak of is that one cult, or cults, that gets under our skin. As a result, that seems to be all that we talk about.

It only brings attention to the wrong things. Besides, Christians need a well-rounded diet. Even good men can go wrong when they turn the focus of the church from Christ to *anything* else - even a hobby horse. Satan does not care what you focus your attention upon as long as it is not Christ.

On the other hand, we may not want to bring undue attention to a cult but we cannot ignore it either. Keep in mind that one of the reasons why cults can subvert believers or overthrow churches is because of ignorance.

> ***Titus 1:10-14*** *For there are many unruly and vain talkers and deceivers, specially they of the circumcision:* ***11*** *Whose mouths must be*

*stopped, who subvert whole houses, teaching things which they ought not, for filthy lucre's sake. **12** One of themselves, even a prophet of their own, said, The Cretians are alway liars, evil beasts, slow bellies. **13** This witness is true. Wherefore rebuke them sharply, that they may be sound in the faith; **14** Not giving heed to Jewish fables, and commandments of men, that turn from the truth.*

As soon as it becomes obvious that a cult organization is seeking to have influence, their heresy must be exposed and expelled.

Dealing With Individuals Who Are in a Cult

Most secular experts agree that cults prey on the following types of people :

- Those who have a strong ***desire to belong*** (this is most people, by the way).

- Those who are ***unassertive*** - the inability to say no or express criticism or doubt. This is tough to measure but some psychologists believe this to be between 25 and 50% of the population.

- Those who tend to be very believing or naive - gullibility (impaired capacity to question critically what one is told, observes, thinks, and so forth).

- Those who are dissatisfied with the status quo.

- Those who are susceptible to trance-like states (in some cases, perhaps, due to prior hallucinogenic drug experiences).

- Those who lack self-confidence.

- Those who have a desire for spiritual meaning.

While we are at it, let's shatter another myth: people who join cults are not stupid, weird, crazy, weak-willed, or neurotic. Many cult members are of above-average intelligence, well-adjusted, adaptable, and perhaps a bit idealistic (http://www.apologeticsindex.org/265-who-joins-cults-and-why).

Anyone is capable of being recruited (or seduced) into a cult if his personal and situational circumstances are right. Currently, there are so many cults formed around so many different types of beliefs that it is impossible for a person to truthfully claim that he would never be vulnerable to a cult's appeal.

In reality, the whole world follows some form of teaching that causes them to be lost – it may be secularism, humanism, etc. But the bottom line is that if we never interact with anyone involved in a cult then no one will hear the gospel.

Just remember, Paul was involved in a cult, and so was every other follower of Judaism in the Bible!

Yet, evangelistic endeavors were very successful because the rules were followed! So what are the rules?

In reality, anyone who does not believe in Christ believes and expresses false teachings. And we must live among, work with, and live with, these same people daily. We simply cannot completely separate from them. And we certainly should never attempt to isolate ourselves completely from them.

If isolation were the correct action, then none would ever hear the Gospel.

Having said that, I want you to notice that God is very concerned about those who call themselves saints.

> ***1 Corinthians 5:9-11*** *I wrote unto you in an epistle not to company with fornicators:* **10** *Yet not altogether with the fornicators of this world, or with the covetous, or extortioners, or with idolaters; for then must ye needs go out of the world.* **11** *But now I have written unto you not to keep company, if any man that is called a brother be a fornicator, or covetous, or an idolater, or a railer, or a drunkard, or an extortioner; with such an one no not to eat.*

A distinction should be made here between the average lost person and the religious lost. We are not to shun the whole world! But we are to separate from those who claim to be saved but will not heed the truth.

> ***Titus 3:9-10*** *But avoid foolish questions, and genealogies, and contentions, and strivings about the law; for they are unprofitable and vain.* **10** *A man that is an heretick after the first and second admonition reject;*

A great many people have been snatched out of the jaws of cults because of a Christian who cared. Sometimes, it takes a while to reach someone – but as long as they are receptive, we should continue working with them.

Cult leaders are people too! They have jobs, go shopping, walk in the park, exercise in the gym, and hang out in coffee shops - just like everyone else. And you will have the opportunity to meet them. So how do you deal with them because, after all, they are the ones who deceive the followers?

First of all, you must ascertain the situation. To say that we will never dialog with a cult leader would not be practical or biblical. Every one of the apostles was involved in a false religious system. Yet they received Christ as their Lord and Saviour and went on to become incredible witnesses for Christ.

Cult leaders can, and sometimes do, leave their groups after their eyes have been opened to their manipulative ways. Case in point: Daniel Shaw, now a psychoanalyst with expertise in cult recovery, was once a member of Heaven's Gate, a cult in Southern California that committed mass suicide in the 1990s.

So let's ask ourselves some pertinent questions before we decide to simply reject or ignore someone who may fit that category:

- ***Did the person approach with the idea of proselytizing?*** We are not to give them the opportunity.

Titus 1:10-11 *For there are many unruly and vain talkers and deceivers, specially they of the circumcision:* ***11*** *Whose mouths must be stopped, who subvert whole houses, teaching things which they ought not, for filthy lucre's sake.*

2 John 1:9-11 *Whosoever transgresseth, and abideth not in the doctrine of Christ, hath not God. He that abideth in the doctrine of Christ, he hath both the Father and the Son.* ***10*** *If there come any unto you, and bring not this doctrine, receive him not into your house, neither bid him God speed:* ***11*** *For he that biddeth him God speed is partaker of his evil deeds.*

- ***Was there a different reason for the meeting?*** Maybe you met them on a bus or spoke with them in a supermarket. Maybe you had to do some form of business with them. Their purpose in speaking with you was not to influence you but for some other reason.

In that case, share the gospel. If the person is reachable, he will recognize the truth. He may not openly acknowledge it, but he will recognize the truth. The simple gospel is more powerful than the best lie.

John 1:5 And the light shineth in darkness; and the darkness comprehended it not.

Also, be aware that there is a difference between a false teacher and an apostate.

Paul was a false teacher. He was also very sincere. He had been blinded to the truth.

Galatians 1:13-14 For ye have heard of my conversation in time past in the Jews' religion, how that beyond measure I persecuted the church of God, and wasted it: 14 And profited in the Jews' religion above many my equals in mine own nation, being more exceedingly zealous of the traditions of my fathers.

Philippians 3:4-6 Though I might also have confidence in the flesh. If any other man thinketh that he hath whereof he might trust in the flesh, I more: 5 Circumcised the eighth day, of the stock of Israel, of the tribe of Benjamin, an Hebrew of the Hebrews; as touching the law, a Pharisee; 6 Concerning zeal, persecuting the church; touching the righteousness which is in the law, blameless.

And yet Paul was marvelously saved.

There is hope for a false teacher. But there is **no** hope for an apostate. He has told God "no" one time too many. He has gone too far.

*Romans 1:21-32 Because that, when they knew **God**, they glorified him not as God, neither were thankful; but became vain in their imaginations, and their foolish heart was darkened. 22 Professing themselves to be wise, they became fools, 23 And changed the glory of* *the uncorruptible God into an image made like to corruptible man, and to birds, and fourfooted beasts, and creeping things. **24** Wherefore God also gave them up to uncleanness through the lusts of their own hearts, to dishonour their own bodies between themselves: **25** Who changed the truth of God into a lie, and worshipped and served the creature more than the Creator, who is blessed for ever. Amen. **26** For this cause God gave them up unto vile affections: for even their women did change the natural use into that which is against nature: **27** And likewise also the men, leaving the natural use of the woman, burned in their lust one toward another; men with men working that which is unseemly, and receiving in themselves that recompence of their error which was meet. **28** And even as they did not like to retain God in their knowledge, God gave them over to a reprobate mind, to do those things which are not convenient; **29** Being filled with all unrighteousness, fornication, wickedness, covetousness, maliciousness; full of envy, murder, debate, deceit, malignity; whisperers, **30** Backbiters, haters of God, despiteful, proud, boasters, inventors of evil things, disobedient to parents, **31** Without understanding, covenantbreakers, without natural affection, implacable, unmerciful: **32** Who knowing the judgment of God, that they which commit such things are worthy of death, not only do the same, but have pleasure in them that do them.*

***Jude 1:11-13** Woe unto them! for they have gone in the way of Cain, and ran greedily after the error of Balaam for reward, and perished in the gainsaying of Core. **12** These are spots in your feasts of charity, when they feast with you, feeding themselves without fear: clouds they are without water, carried about of winds; trees whose fruit withereth, without fruit, twice dead, plucked up by the roots; **13** Raging waves of the sea, foaming out their own shame; wandering stars, to whom is reserved the blackness of darkness for ever.*

Dealing With a Recovering Cult Follower

Jude 1:22 *And of some have compassion, making a difference:*

Most of us know that salvation is just the beginning of the Christian walk. Thus, when a person gets saved from a cult environment, it takes a lot of time and patience to bring them to a point of biblical thinking.

You may be faced with the task of teaching and reteaching for many years before the truth can sink in. I call it unraveling the carpet. Before you can get to one point, you first must undo something else.

Many former cult followers will still have certain prejudices, superstitions, and fears which may take years to overcome.

One influence of cult teaching is the idea that certain people are better than others. This is a subtle philosophy that is ingrained in many cult members by their leadership in order to bring about a separation of the cult members from the rest of society. Thus, even after a person comes out of the cult, it may take a good deal of time for them to see the pridefulness of their thinking.

Sometimes a former cult follower will believe that one particular place is superior to another. For example, a former Jew may have an unusually high reverence for Jerusalem. Or, a Moslem may have a high reverence for Mecca.

It is difficult to define this area or to cite examples due to the incredible amount of superstitious influences that can arise in cults.

One of the biggest areas that a former cult follower will need to deal with is the area of loss:

Janja Lalich sensed something was "off" about the group she'd joined. They controlled her income and cut her off from her family. She was ordered to pick a new name, burn her belongings and spy on new members. When her mother was dying and Lalich wanted to spend time with her, she was called to the carpet and criticized for being "selfish." She was expected to work 17- to 18-hour days for "the party," forsaking all other pursuits. (http://www.religionnewsblog.com/8605/ the-power-of-cults)

A former cult follower may be dealing with regrets related to the **loss of time**. We speak of redeeming the time and a sensitive Christian will want to do that.

But it can take years to come to grips with time lost or wasted on the wrong priorities and that can be difficult to accept.

Sometimes, as a result of demands forced upon a former cult follower, there may also be a **loss of finances**. In other words, they have come to understand just how much of a financial drain their particular cult had upon them and they will regret it.

One of the saddest regrets is that often, there can be the **loss of family**. Sometimes the cult follower led the family into the cult and now wants to get them out.

Sometimes a family will disown them for leaving the cult. This happens with Jewish, Muslim, or Catholic families very frequently.

Sometimes a cult will demand that a person leave their family. In some cases, the loss of contact has been so severe that they may not even know where their families are. This is often the case with followers of Sun Myoung Moon or Hare Krishnas.

Sometimes a cult will require its members to "marry". The Unification Church, led by Sun Myung Moon, is known for conducting mass weddings where thousands of couples participate simultaneously. These events, often referred to as "Blessing Ceremonies," aim to promote the idea of creating ideal families. [1]

There can be issues with a ***loss of morality***. There are groups or organizations where leaders exploit followers sexually, often involving manipulation, coercion, or abuse.

Several high-profile cases involving allegations of sexual exploitation within groups have received public attention in recent years, contributing to increased awareness of such issues. Some examples: Warren Jeffs and the Fundamental Church of Latter-Day Saints who still practice polygamy; David Berg and the Children of God (he offered them all the sex they wanted); Keith Raniere and NXIVM (he used nude photography to control his female followers).

There may be struggles with ***loss of identity***. "Loss of identity" refers to a state where an individual experiences a diminished sense of self, often accompanied by feelings of confusion, disconnection, or a perceived erosion of one's unique characteristics, values, or personal identity.

This may be brought about through submersion into extreme cultural abnormalities, relocation, sleep deprivation, trauma, or crisis of values.

There can be a ***loss of social skills***. This can be caused by a variety of issues such as social isolation, depression, lack of meaningful communication, physical or mental abuse, or substance abuse.

And of course, as a result of withdrawal from culturally accepted norms, there may also be the ***loss of education and job skills***. Let's face it, there are cults and world religions that are fairly well accepted in society, and generally speaking, these people can be associates in the workplace without too much discomfort for others.

But then, there are others that we simply feel uncomfortable being around. This group typically finds it difficult to keep employment.

The bottom line is that there is no single answer to meeting all of these issues. One must prayerfully seek to help a recovering cult follower to integrate back into a normal life. This often takes a lot of time and can be very trying.

But in the end, it is also very rewarding!

Dealing With Cult Influences in Your Church

Make no mistake, the more of an impact a church has in a community, the greater the possibility that a cult member will seek to infiltrate your church.

I know it sounds conspiratorial, but it is a known practice among cults. They will come in and then seek:

- To corrupt the church

- To reduce it effectiveness

- To cause its demise

- Or, to convert it from the inside.

Acts 20:28-31 Take heed therefore unto yourselves, and to all the flock, over the which the Holy Ghost hath made you overseers, to feed the church of God, which he hath purchased with his own blood. 29 For I know this, that after my departing shall grievous wolves enter in among you, not sparing the flock. 30 Also of your own selves shall men arise, speaking perverse things, to draw away disciples after them. 31 Therefore watch, and remember, that by the space of three years I ceased not to warn every one night and day with tears.

An interesting point that many people do not understand is that many cults began with leaders who did not intentionally seek to mislead the people:

- Jim Jones began as a Methodist lay preacher who left his church because they refused to integrate blacks into the congregation.

- David (Moses) Berg of the Children of God started with the Missionary Alliance Church, which, although they are not doctrinally sound, is certainly not a cult.

An evangelistic church will have a variety of people from all walks of life in their midst. So the probability of having influences in your church from those who are, or were, involved in a cult is high.

I t may be that a certain cult mentality is already prevalent in your church and if you study the situation, you may very well find the culprit.

Of course, I have known for a long time that there is sectarianism (excessive attachment to a group or sect) in the church. It has always been that way.

1 Corinthians 1:10 Now I beseech you, brethren, by the name of our Lord Jesus Christ, that ye all speak the same thing, and that there be no divisions among you; but that ye be perfectly joined together in the same mind and in the same judgment.

But it is hard to combat this way of thinking when those who advocate it are much more faithful to church attendance than the average church member.

But this is typically the case.

Now, these are not carte-blanche rules for identifying cult influence in a church because these conditions may exist for other reasons as well. But here are some signs, that if you can identify them, there is a need to look deeper:

- Members who express a deep devotion and love to the church or leader but do not demonstrate this same love and devotion to the Lord nor demonstrate empathy for others.

- An overemphasis on emotional highs during the service by members who are not spiritual any other time!

- Cliques are organized around a certain personality in the congregation.

- Both positive and negative peer pressure are designed to bring individuals into compliance with the actions of the group.

There has been more than one case of leaders who have intentionally taken an otherwise good church down the path to cultism. There are signs when this is happening too.

Cult leaders tend to *emphasize some special relationship they presume to have with God*. For example:

• David Koresh believed he was some sort of Messiah.

• Sun Myung Moon believed his name is somehow prophetic and he is in some way, "the Word made clear". He died in 2012 so I guess that didn't work out so well for him!

• Joseph Smith claimed to be some kind of modern prophet who would restore Christianity.

Cult leaders often *claim to have extraordinary knowledge* of spiritual truth.

In the beginning, they seem innocent. They open the Bible one day and it "speaks out" to them in a way that hasn't been heard before (but cannot be confirmed by other Scriptures).

Or, on the subjective side, "God" speaks to them, telling them something remarkable. They do not feel accountable to the Scriptures for their newfound "discoveries" because they have heard directly from God!

Eventually, these leaders *believe they have special privileges* that are above everyone else. They can have more than one wife, various sexual encounters, complete control over finances, or live in luxury while their followers struggle and sacrifice.

Cult leaders, in every situation, and varying degrees, *must exercise control*. Scriptures like Hebrews 13:17; Psalm 105:15, etc. are used to manipulate the member and justify the leader's position. These verses are taken out of context and were never intended to make leaders unaccountable.

The leader/leadership often determines the areas of your life that are important for you to submit in. Refusing their counsel is to be rebellious. In many cases, the use of guilt, fear, or even confessed secrets are used to control individuals.

Measures of Protection

Acts 20:28-31 Take heed therefore unto yourselves, and to all the flock, over the which the Holy Ghost hath made you overseers, to feed the church of God, which he hath purchased with his own blood. 29 For I know this, that after my departing shall grievous wolves enter in among you, not sparing the flock. 30 Also of your own selves shall men arise, speaking perverse things, to draw away disciples after them. 31 Therefore watch, and remember, that by the space of three years I ceased not to warn every one night and day with tears.

"Take heed". In other words, be careful. Be careful personally and be careful as a church. There will be intruders. And there will be those on the inside already who will seek to destroy the church.

And understand that the devil is no fool. He doesn't waste his time on churches or individuals that pose no threat to his plans. He will specifically target the ones who are making a difference.

So, knowing this is true, there are some things that we must be doing.

We must not lose our desire to reach the lost. This will be an open door of opportunity for the cults to infiltrate. But we are called to separate ourselves, not isolate ourselves.

If we do not evangelize, we will not be meeting the great commission, but at the same time, evangelism has its inherent dangers.

We cannot get into the business of "targeting" a certain group or avoiding another group. Every soul is a perspective soldier recruit!

We must not lose our diligence to defend the church. We do this with sound teaching so that the current members will be equipped doctrinally to defend themselves.

This is important because cults (actually, the devil using his false apostles) prey on those who are unstable in the faith – it does not matter if they are new believers or un-studious.

This will also help if the time ever comes when a doctrinal dispute arises in the church. Be on the offensive by explaining why certain doctrines are heretical.

We need to ensure there is ***proper hermeneutics*** because false teachers twist the scriptures.

2 Peter 3:16 As also in all his epistles, speaking in them of these things; in which are some things hard to be understood, which they that are unlearned and unstable wrest, as they do also the other scriptures, unto their own destruction.

The teaching of the Scriptures must be handled accurately, fully, and exclusively.

2 Timothy 2:15 Study to shew thyself approved unto God, a workman that needeth not to be ashamed, rightly dividing the word of truth.

Acts 20:27 For I have not shunned to declare unto you all the counsel of God.

Galatians 1:8 But though we, or an angel from heaven, preach any other gospel unto you than that which we have preached unto you, let him be accursed.

We must also have a ***properly constructed theology*** because false teachers lack understanding.

Colossians 2:18 Let no man beguile you of your reward in a voluntary humility and worshipping of angels, intruding into those things which he hath not seen, vainly puffed up by his fleshly mind,

Every person approaches Scripture with a pre-conceived theology. This applies to everyone - Pharisees, Apostles, even Christ.[2]

Matthew 16:2 He answered and said unto them, When it is evening, ye say, It will be fair weather: for the sky is red.

Acts 5:28 Saying, Did not we straitly command you that ye should not teach in this name? and, behold, ye have filled Jerusalem with your doctrine, and intend to bring this man's blood upon us.

Matthew 7:28 And it came to pass, when Jesus had ended these sayings, the people were astonished at his doctrine:

But to have a good system of beliefs you must study!

2 Timothy 2:15 Study to shew thyself approved unto God, a workman that needeth not to be ashamed, rightly dividing the word of truth.

2 Timothy 3:14-17 But continue thou in the things which thou hast learned and hast been assured of, knowing of whom thou hast learned them; 15 And that from a child thou hast known the holy scriptures, which are able to make thee wise unto salvation through faith which is in Christ Jesus. 16 All scripture is given by inspiration of God, and is profitable for doctrine, for reproof, for correction, for instruction in righteousness: 17 That the man of God may be perfect, throughly furnished unto all good works.

If the doctrinal position of any group places the mode of salvation in the hands of man, it qualifies as a cult.

Titus 3:5 Not by works of righteousness which we have done, but according to his mercy he saved us, by the washing of regeneration, and renewing of the Holy Ghost;

There are several methods by which this is employed:

• By underrating the powers of Christ not only to save but also to intercede.

• By adding stipulations that we must perform before Calvary can be effectual.

• By assuming that Christ was not God in the flesh.

Take note that what we are speaking of, in each case, is an attack upon the doctrine of Christology. And this is always the case for if Christ is who the Scriptures teach, then a system of works cannot co-exist. Therefore every cult teaching must belittle Christ in some way.

Cults - How Do We Handle Them?

Titus 1:10-11 *For there are many unruly and vain talkers and deceivers, specially they of the circumcision:* ***11*** *Whose mouths must be stopped, who subvert whole houses, teaching things which they ought not, for filthy lucre's sake.*

Titus 3:9-10 *But avoid foolish questions, and genealogies, and contentions, and strivings about the law; for they are unprofitable and vain.* ***10*** *A man that is an heretick after the first and second admonition reject;*

You are faced with false teaching daily. This is a reality. We face it in media, education, and business, to name a few sources among many. Much of its teaching cannot be avoided. In this case, God grants grace to overcome.

But sometimes we knowingly partake of false teaching. In this case, we have sinned and stand responsible before God.

Far too often it would appear that Christians have the idea that the way to defend our churches and families is with biting words. However, it is Christ who has promised to protect the church from false doctrine.

> *Revelation 2:14 But I have a few things against thee, because thou hast there them that hold the doctrine of Balaam, who taught Balac to cast a stumblingblock before the children of Israel, to eat things sacrificed unto idols, and to commit fornication.*

> *Revelation 2:16 Repent; or else I will come unto thee quickly, and will fight against them with the sword of my mouth.*

> *Revelation 2:20-23 Notwithstanding I have a few things against thee, because thou sufferest that woman Jezebel, which calleth herself a prophetess, to teach and to seduce my servants to commit fornication, and to eat things sacrificed unto idols. 21 And I gave her space to repent of her fornication; and she repented not. 22 Behold, I will cast her into a bed, and them that commit adultery with her into great tribulation, except they repent of their deeds. 23 And I will kill her children with death; and all the churches shall know that I am he which searcheth the reins and hearts: and I will give unto every one of you according to your works.*

Our responsibility is to remain true to the scriptures. We are not to allow those who believe false doctrine to remain as if they are one of the brethren.

> *Revelation 2:14-16 But I have a few things against thee, because thou hast there them that hold the doctrine of Balaam, who taught*

*Balac to cast a stumblingblock before the children of Israel, to eat things sacrificed unto idols, and to commit fornication. **15** So hast thou also them that hold the doctrine of the Nicolaitans, which thing I hate. **16** Repent; or else I will come unto thee quickly, and will fight against them with the sword of my mouth.*

We are not to allow false teaching to occur.

***Revelation 2:20-23** Notwithstanding I have a few things against thee, because thou sufferest that woman Jezebel, which calleth herself a prophetess, to teach and to seduce my servants to commit fornication, and to eat things sacrificed unto idols. **21** And I gave her space to repent of her fornication; and she repented not. **22** Behold, I will cast her into a bed, and them that commit adultery with her into great tribulation, except they repent of their deeds. **23** And I will kill her children with death; and all the churches shall know that I am he which searcheth the reins and hearts: and I will give unto every one of you according to your works.*

If we will be true to God's Word, and handle cults in a scriptural way, then Christ will handle the rest of the details.

Yet, at the same time, we have been given the charge to "contend for the faith". In doing so, what should we do and what should we not do?

Most Christians take the matter of dealing with cults very seriously but very few know how to deal with them. They tend to go to two extremes which are both unbiblical.

They may go the route of isolation. But how can we reach them if we ignore them?

Or they may go to the opposite extreme of full reception. This is the other extreme that must also be avoided.

Common Mistakes We Make When Discussing Other Religions

One of the major mistakes we make is that far too often we ***insult instead of edify***. Yet the Bible tells us that our words ought not to be this way:

Colossians 4:6 Let your speech be alway with grace, seasoned with salt, that ye may know how ye ought to answer every man.

Sometimes we employ ***the use of derogatory terms*** which only serve to build barriers. They are offensive to cult members. They are offensive to Christians who know better.

Insults show that you are full of pride. Insults show a lack of compassion. Insults show a lack of true substantial teaching. Insults never win anyone over to your side of the argument. And if we are to seek to win them, how does this help in any way?

More than once I have seen well-meaning Christians approach cult groups with the idea that they will denounce their activities. And yet they approach them ***without any knowledge of the Scriptures*** and end up causing more harm than good.

1 Peter 3:15 But sanctify the Lord God in your hearts: and be ready always to give an answer to every man that asketh you a reason of the hope that is in you with meekness and fear:

First of all, if you don't know what the Bible says, how can you be sure you are right?

It is fruitless to tell someone that they are wrong without telling them why. Many who are involved in cults are quite intellectual. They are going to demand more than a "blanket" arbitrary statement.

One of the major mistakes that people make when dealing with cults is to ***attack the symptoms*** but not the sickness.

2 Timothy 2:23-26 But foolish and unlearned questions avoid, knowing that they do gender strifes. 24 And the servant of the Lord *must not strive; but be gentle unto all men, apt to teach, patient, **25** In meekness instructing those that oppose themselves; if God peradventure will give them repentance to the acknowledging of the truth; **26** And that they may recover themselves out of the snare of the devil, who are taken captive by him at his will.*

***2 Peter 3:15-18** And account that the longsuffering of our Lord is salvation; even as our beloved brother Paul also according to the wisdom given unto him hath written unto you; **16** As also in all his epistles, speaking in them of these things; in which are some things hard to be understood, which they that are unlearned and unstable wrest, as they do also the other scriptures, unto their own destruction. **17** Ye therefore, beloved, seeing ye know these things before, beware lest ye also, being led away with the error of the wicked, fall from your own stedfastness. **18** But grow in grace, and in the knowledge of our Lord and Saviour Jesus Christ. To him be glory both now and for ever. Amen.*

If you tell a Catholic that it is useless to pray to Mary but never show them from the Scriptures that Jesus is the only mediator between God and man, you have accomplished nothing. It is merely a useless and often prideful argument.

Convincing a Muslim that it is okay to eat beef but never tell him about the Bread of Life, you haven't accomplished anything. He is still lost without Christ.

A fifth mistake that is often made is when we debate a cult follower with well-known Christian expressions but ***never define the terms***.

Cults, especially those who refer to themselves as "Bible-based", are very good at redefining biblical terms. In effect, they are wresting the Scriptures.

***2 Peter 3:16** As also in all his epistles, speaking in them of these things; in which are some things hard to be understood, which they that are unlearned and unstable wrest, as they do also the other scriptures, unto their own destruction.*

For example, the Mormons will say that they believe Jesus is God; but in actuality, they believe Jesus attained godhood. Thus, they deny the Trinity. The average believer would have a hard time disputing the Mormons because he thinks they are saying the same things!

A careful believer should not discuss the Scriptures in theological terms. He should define his terms and force the cultists to do the same. Once they define their terms, then you can more clearly see the difference in beliefs.

The average cult thrives on ignorance and many of those involved in cults sincerely don't see a difference between what the cult teaches and what the Bible says.

2 Peter 2:14 Having eyes full of adultery, and that cannot cease from sin; beguiling unstable souls: an heart they have exercised with covetous practices; cursed children:

Take note that the word "beguiling" is not an adjective to describe unstable souls. No, it is a verb. The false teacher beguiles unstable souls. And an unstable soul does not have a solid foundation.

Walter Martin states,

"And just as the American Bar Association will not tolerate confusion of terminology in the trial of cases, and as the American Medical Association will not tolerate redefinition of terminology in diagnostic and surgical medicine, so also the church of Jesus Christ has every right not to tolerate the gross perversions and redefinitions of historical, biblical terminology simply to accommodate a culture and a society that cannot tolerate an absolute standard or criterion of truth, even if it be revealed by God in His Word and through the true witness of His Spirit." (Kingdom of the Cults)

World Religions (As Versus Cults)

World Religions	Number of Adherents
Christianity	2.1 billion
Islam	1.5 billion
Hinduism	900 million
Secular/Nonreligious/Agnostic/Atheist	850 million
Buddhism	360 million
Chinese traditional religion	225 million
Primal-indigenous	190 million
Yoruba religion	20 million
Juche	19 million
Sikhism	18 million
Judaism	15 million
Spiritism	14 million
Babi and Bahai faiths	6 million
Jainism	4 million
Shinto	4 million
Cao Dai	3 million
Tenrikyo	2.4 million
Neo-Paganism	1 million
Unitarian-Universalism	800 thousand
Scientology	750 thousand
Rastafarianism	700 thousand
Zoroastrianism	150 thousand

. . . .

AS WE BEGIN TO TAKE a closer look at various cults, we must continually remind ourselves that the only measuring stick that we can legitimately use is the Bible itself. In short, never lose sight of the truth that the Bible is the sole authority of faith and practice.

The History of Buddhism

Buddhism is the second oldest of all present false religions. It originated in India with Siddartha Gautama.

Siddartha Gautama (c. 560 B.C.) was the prince of the Kaya tribe of North India. He was raised in luxury and wealth, but at the age of 29 abandoned his wife and son to search out the reason why pain and suffering exist in the world.

He lived the life of an aesthetic (not uncommon at the time) for seven years searching for truth.

At age 36, he was sitting under a Bodhi tree when he suddenly obtained "Nirvana" [3] upon which he took on the title "Buddha", or "the Enlightened One".[4] While under this tree, he claimed to realize the "Four Noble Truths" which would form the basic premise of Buddhism.

Buddhism has spread from India throughout Southeast Asia and has even accumulated followers in the West. It has about 360 million adherents worldwide.[5] There are 3-4 million followers in the United States alone. In 2020, approximately 22-23% of the South Korean population identified as Buddhists.

Buddhists of today have adopted modern Christian practices such as Sunday schools, tracts, and even financing missions to the West.

Buddhism in Korea. [6]

IN A.D. 372, IT WAS introduced into the Koguryo Dynasty from China by the Chinese monk Soonto. Soosoorim, King of Kogoryu, built two monasteries for Soonto and committed his son to be trained as a Buddhist.

The Baekje Dynasty, not wanting to be outdone by Kogoryu, sent for Marananda, an Indian Buddhist. The Silla Dynasty accepted Buddhism forty years later from the missionary Meukhoja.

By A.D. 424, all three dynasties had proclaimed Buddhism the religion of the state. Buddhism began to flourish as a "worldly" form of religion that

encouraged music, literature, and dance to express the meaning of Buddhism.
[7]

The most popular variety of Buddhism was Buddhism combined with Shamanism. Many of the Buddhist monks danced, sang, and performed the rituals of the Shamans.

In 525, the King of the Silla kingdom and the King of the Baekje kingdom passed laws against killing animals for food and commanded that the kingdom adhere to the Buddhist Eight Commandments.[8] In 599, all the fishing tackle was confiscated, and all imprisoned birds were set free.

Korean Buddhists evangelize other nations.[9]

STARTING IN A.D. 545, the King of Baekje and Silla sent Buddhist missionaries and nuns to Japan. When China lost the religion of Buddhism due to severe persecution, Korean Buddhists resuscitated the religion and sent many books and missionaries to China. China and Japan both owe their Buddhism to Korea.

Buddhism was the predominant religion of Korea up to five hundred years ago. But by the end of the Koryo period (1349), Buddhism was restricted and Confucianism replaced Buddhism as the state religion of Korea. The Yi dynasty continued the persecution of the Buddhists.[10]

A feast was given in honor of two hundred Buddhist monks in 1865. This was the first time in two hundred years that a formal recognition of Buddhism was given by any Korean ruler. It was also the last time.

Communism in North Korea and the Christian movement in South Korea have greatly hampered the growth of Buddhism.

Yet, at the same time, old traditions and ancient temples are still guarded and preserved.

Koreans most commonly call Buddha *Shakyamuni* ("Saint/Teacher of the House of Sakya"), *Sakayerai* ("the Coming One of the House of Sakya"), or *Seichon* ("World Honored One").

Modern forms of Buddhism

HINAYANA,[1] Lesser Vehicle, (Theravada): Emphasizes the writings of the Buddha, the closest to Buddha's original teachings, in southern Asia, Sri Lanka, Burma, Thailand, and Cambodia.

Mahayana,[2] Greater Vehicle: emphasizes the spirit of Buddha, by far the largest branch of Buddhism, in China, Japan, Tibet, Korea, Nepal, Indonesia, Vietnam, Sri Lanka, and Thailand.

Mahayana introduced the doctrine of *"bodhisattva"*, *"helpers"*: Enlightened perfect beings, who choose to help others reincarnate, instead of entering Nirvana (i.e. the Dalai Lama).

With this doctrine, Mahayana makes a god out of the Buddha and out of anyone enlightened, in open rebellion against the teachings of Gautama Buddha.

Vajrayana, the Diamond Vehicle, and the Third Vehicle, *Tantrism*. It borrows the Hindu belief in the goddess Shakti's sexual power and developed a cult devoted to idols, magic, and sex. It has been condemned as a degeneration of Buddhism, and indeed it is an anti-Buddhist philosophy.

Tibetan Buddhism: In Tibet and Japan, added to Tantrism the primitive animistic religions of Tibet, the magic "bon", and some "Mahayana" doctrines to create the most open occultist of all Eastern religions. It created the super-authority of the *"Dalai Lama"*, a god-on-earth, heading a hierarchy of priests, destroying the "religion without authority" that Gautama the Buddha proposed.

Zen Buddhism, from Japan, had become in the mid-20th century perhaps the best-known of the Buddhist schools in the Western world. "Zen" means "be nothing, think nothing", and "Zazen" "seated meditation"; its adherents claim Zen to be the quintessential of Buddhism.

Nichiren Buddhism: In the 13th century a Japanese, Nichiren, founded a school whose aims are the opposite of Gautama Buddha: To satisfy all desires, because "happy individuals can build a happy world"; with emphasis on acquiring wealth, power, personal happiness, political power.

---

1. http://religion-cults.com/Eastern/Buddhism/budis6.htm

2.   http://religion-cults.com/Eastern/Buddhism/budis6.htm

Pure Land (***Sukhavati, Jodo, Ching-tu***): One enters the Pure Land through faith in the god Amitabha, or Amida or Buddha, by repeating the "nembutsu", "Namu-Amida-Butsu", "Have faith in Amida, and you will be saved", they proclaim, imitating Jesus Christ. In a total contradiction to the teachings of the Buddha.

Hinduism: The Buddha, for the Hindus, is the 9th incarnation of Vishnu. Of course, openly against the will and teachings of Gautama Buddha himself. The 7th and 8th incarnations of Vishnu for the Hindus are Rama and Krishna, and the 10th incarnation and the last one will be "Kalkin", still to come.[11]

Four Major Teachings of Buddhism

BUDDHA CALLED THEM his "Four Noble Truths". By adhering to these "truths" one could obtain Nirvana and peace. These "Four Noble Truths" formed the basis for Buddhism.

The truth of suffering - Buddha said that existence is pain, hence, because we suffer, we know that we exist.

The truth of the cause of suffering - Buddha said that we suffer because we have desires, and we have desires because we are ignorant.

The truth of the cessation of suffering - Buddha says that when suffering is destroyed, then Nirvana is obtained.

The truth of the way to remove suffering - Buddha says is by a noble, "Eight-fold Path of Righteousness". (righteous views, right intentions, right speech, right livelihood, right effort, right mindfulness, right concentrations, and right action—good works!

The Eight-Fold Path of Righteousness:

1. ***Right View*** – Accept the Four Noble Truths.
2. ***Right Resolve*** – Renouncing all desires and any thoughts like lust, bitterness, and cruelty, and must harm no living creature.
3. ***Right Speech***—Speaking only truth. There can be no lying, slander, or vain talk.
4. ***Right Behavior***—One must abstain from sexual immorality, stealing, and all killing.

5. ***Right Occupation***—Working in an occupation that benefits others and harms no one.
6. ***Right Effort*** - Seeking to eliminate any evil qualities within and prevent any new ones from arising. One should seek to attain good and moral qualities and develop those already possessed. Seek to grow in maturity and perfection until universal love is attained.
7. ***Right Contemplation*** - Being observant, contemplative, and free of desire and sorrow.
8. ***Right Meditation*** - After freeing oneself of all desires and evil, a person must concentrate his efforts on meditation so that he can overcome any sensation of pleasure or pain enter a state of transcending consciousness, and attain a state of perfection. Buddhists believe that through self-effort one can attain the eternal state of nirvana.

Biblical Truth versus the "Four Noble Truths":

THE TRUTH OF SUFFERING - God says that we exist, so we exist! (we don't have to burn our fingers on fire to know that we exist, God says it and we believe it)

The truth of the cause of suffering - God says that we suffer because of our wickedness and sin. Had Adam and Eve never eaten the fruit, we would never have known suffering.

The truth of the cessation of suffering - God says that suffering is destroyed when we reach our home in heaven.

The truth of the way to remove suffering - God says that we cannot remove our suffering through our good works, but only by his grace.

Seven Major Problems with Buddhism.

1. ***Buddhism propagates the idea of intellectual enlightenment as a way of self-salvation*** and therefore rejects the necessity for a Savior.

Buddhism demands that man look within himself for the answer to salvation. This is contrary to biblical teaching concerning the corruption of fallen man.

Romans 3:10-18 *As it is written, There is none righteous, no, not one: 11 There is none that understandeth, there is none that seeketh after God. 12 They are all gone out of the way, they are together become unprofitable; there is none that doeth good, no, not one. 13 Their throat is an open sepulchre; with their tongues they have used deceit; the poison of asps is under their lips: 14 Whose mouth is full of cursing and bitterness: 15 Their feet are swift to shed blood: 16 Destruction and misery are in their ways: 17 And the way of peace have they not known: 18 There is no fear of God before their eyes.*

Romans 5:12 *Wherefore, as by one man sin entered into the world, and death by sin; and so death passed upon all men, for that all have sinned:*

1 Corinthians 2:5 states that faith should be based not on man's wisdom, but on the power of God. God specifically says not to trust in man.

1 Corinthians 3:18-21 *Let no man deceive himself. If any man among you seemeth to be wise in this world, let him become a fool, that he may be wise. 19 For the wisdom of this world is foolishness with God. For it is written, He taketh the wise in their own craftiness. 20 And again, The Lord knoweth the thoughts of the wise, that they are vain. 21 Therefore let no man glory in men. For all things are yours;*

Without a Savior, all is lost.

1 Peter 2:24 *Who his own self bare our sins in his own body on the tree, that we, being dead to sins, should live unto righteousness: by whose stripes ye were healed.*

1 John 2:2 *And he is the propitiation for our sins: and not for ours only, but also for the sins of the whole world.*

Salvation is not a way that we must somehow find, but a person in whom we place our trust (John 14:6).

2. Because Buddhism propagates self-enlightenment, it ***logically denies the existence of God***. This is why Buddhists worship Buddha; for them, there is no God – only a state of nirvana.

Psalm 36:1 and Psalm 53:1 states that it is foolish to think there is no God. 1 Corinthians 3:19 says that the wisdom of the world is foolishness with God.

3. Buddhism ***asserts that good works bring about happiness***, and this happiness is the foundation for salvation. The Bible teaches salvation is by faith and that works cannot bring about salvation.

> ***Romans 4:4-5*** *Now to him that worketh is the reward not reckoned of grace, but of debt.* ***5*** *But to him that worketh not, but believeth on him that justifieth the ungodly, his faith is counted for righteousness.*

> ***Titus 3:5*** *Not by works of righteousness which we have done, but according to his mercy he saved us, by the washing of regeneration, and renewing of the Holy Ghost;*

> ***Ephesians 2:8-9*** *For by grace are ye saved through faith; and that not of yourselves: it is the gift of God:* ***9*** *Not of works, lest any man should boast.*

The only foundation for salvation is Jesus Christ.

> ***Acts 4:12*** *Neither is there salvation in any other: for there is none other name under heaven given among men, whereby we must be saved.*

4. Buddhism ***dismisses the idea of sin due to the absence of an absolute standard of law and holiness***. 1 John 1:8,10 says that to think that sin doesn't exist is to deceive one's self.

> ***1 John 1:8*** *If we say that we have no sin, we deceive ourselves, and the truth is not in us.*

> ***1 John 1:10*** *If we say that we have not sinned, we make him a liar, and his word is not in us.*

5. Buddhism ***asserts that it will open one's eyes***. The Bible says that all men are blind until God opens their eyes.

> ***2 Corinthians 4:4*** *In whom the god of this world hath blinded the minds of them which believe not, lest the light of the glorious gospel of Christ, who is the image of God, should shine unto them.*

6. Buddhism ***distorts the reason for suffering***.
The Bible says that men's sorrow is multiplied because of disobedience and sin.

> ***Genesis 3:16-19*** *Unto the woman he said, I will greatly multiply thy sorrow and thy conception; in sorrow thou shalt bring forth children; and thy desire shall be to thy husband, and he shall rule over thee. **17** And unto Adam he said, Because thou hast hearkened unto the voice of thy wife, and hast eaten of the tree, of which I commanded thee, saying, Thou shalt not eat of it: cursed is the ground for thy sake; in sorrow shalt thou eat of it all the days of thy life; **18** Thorns also and thistles shall it bring forth to thee; and thou shalt eat the herb of the field; **19** In the sweat of thy face shalt thou eat bread, till thou return unto the ground; for out of it wast thou taken: for dust thou art, and unto dust shalt thou return.*

The Bible also teaches that sometimes suffering has an eternal purpose in contrast to man's judgments.

> ***John 9:1-3*** *And as Jesus passed by, he saw a man which was blind from his birth. **2** And his disciples asked him, saying, Master, who did sin, this man, or his parents, that he was born blind? **3** Jesus answered, Neither hath this man sinned, nor his parents: but that the works of God should be made manifest in him.*

7. Buddhism ***denies the existence of a soul***.

> *"This is the defining premise of Buddhism and one of the main things that differentiates it from other religions. In ancient Hinduism, the*

soul was called the atman and the basic Buddhist view was described as anatman—no soul." (https://www.lionsroar.com/do-buddhists-believe-in-a-soul/)

1 Thessalonians 5:23 states the existence of three distinct parts of man, one of which is the soul.

__1 Thessalonians 5:23__ And the very God of peace sanctify you wholly; and I pray God your whole spirit and soul and body be preserved blameless unto the coming of our Lord Jesus Christ.

Although Buddhism adheres to the belief in karma and rebirth, the Bible says that after death is the judgment.

__Hebrews 9:27__ And as it is appointed unto men once to die, but after this the judgment:

__Revelation 20:14-15__ And death and hell were cast into the lake of fire. This is the second death. __15__ And whosoever was not found written in the book of life was cast into the lake of fire.

The History of Confucianism

"Confucius says,

- "Man who runs behind a car soon gets exhausted".

- "Man who open car door for girlfriend reveal one thing: either car is new or girlfriend is new."

- "Behind every successful man is good woman'and very surprised mother-in-law."

- "No husband ever been shot while he do dishes."

- "Man who cut himself while shaving lose face."

- "Man who keep both feet firmly planted on ground have trouble putting on pants."

For a man who is so often quoted, it is interesting that the originator of Confucianism may not have actually written anything! Modern scholars are divided as to whether Confucius wrote his teachings down or whether they were compiled later by his followers.

We do know that after his death, his followers compiled his teachings into The *Analects*,[12] which lay out Confucius' ethical system.

Confucius (K'ung-fu-tzu, literally "Master Kung," 551 B.C. - 479 B.C.) was a Chinese philosopher whose doctrine still has great influence on the social and religious culture of China, Japan, Korea, and Vietnam. Interestingly, while Confucius was peddling his form of heresy in China, Gautama was peddling his heresy in India (560 BC)!

His philosophy emphasized personal and governmental morality, the correctness of social relationships, justice, and sincerity.

His teachings became more popular than the prevailing philosophies of Legalism, and Taoism during the Han Dynasty (206 BC. - AD. 220).

Confucius' teachings were introduced to Europe by the Jesuit Matteo Ricci, who was the first to Latinize the name "Confucius". His teachings are known primarily through the Analects of Confucius, which were written after his death.

Written during the Spring and Autumn Period[13] through the Warring States Period (479 - 221 BC.), "The Analects" is the representative work of Confucianism and continues to have a tremendous influence on Chinese and East Asian thought and values today.

Modern historians do not believe that any specific documents can be said to have been written by Confucius, but for nearly 2,000 years he was thought to be the editor or author of all the Five Classics such as the Classic of Rites, and the Spring and Autumn Annals.

Confucius was born in 551 BC in the city of Qufu, in the Chinese State of Lu (now part of Shandong Province). According to an ancient Chinese history book, The Records of the Grand Historian, written 109 – 91 BC, Confucius was conceived out of wedlock.

His father was seventy, and his mother was only eighteen at his birth. His father died when he was three, and he was brought up in poverty by his mother. Confucius worked as a shepherd, cowherd, clerk, and bookkeeper.

When Confucius was twenty-three, his mother died and he entered three years of mourning.

As a young man, he became an administrative manager in the State of Lu and rose to the position of Justice Minister. However, he resigned after two years because he disapproved of the politics of his authorities.

He then began a series of journeys around the small kingdoms of north-central China where he espoused his political beliefs but did not see them implemented.

At sixty-eight, he returned home and spent his last years teaching disciples from a set of books called the Five Classics. Greatly affected by the grief of losing both his son and his favorite disciples, he died at the age of 72.

The Five Classics (Wujing)

THE FIVE CLASSICS, also called "Wujing" are five ancient Chinese books used by Confucianism as the basis of studies. According to tradition, they were compiled or edited by Confucius himself.

These books consist of:

The Classic of Changes or I Ching - a manual of divination based on the eight trigrams attributed to the mythical emperor Fu Xi. (By Confucius' time these eight trigrams had been multiplied to sixty-four hexagrams.) The I Ching is still used by adherents of folk religion.

The Classic of Poetry or The Book of Odes - made up of 305 poems of folk songs, festal songs which were traditionally sung at court festivities and ceremonies, and eulogies which were sung at sacrifices to gods and ancestral spirits of the royal house. This book is traditionally credited as a compilation from Confucius.

The Classic of Rites - social forms and ceremonies. A restoration of a writing called the Lijing, lost in the third century B.C. It describes ancient rites and court ceremonies.

The Classic of History - A collection of documents and speeches alleged to have been written by rulers and officials of the early Zhou period and before. It contains examples of early Chinese prose.

Spring and Autumn Annals - A historical record of the state of Lu, Confucius' native state, from 722 B.C. to 479 B.C. written (or edited) by Confucius, with implied condemnation of usurpations, murder, incest, etc.

There exists the ***Classic of Music*** which is sometimes referred to as the sixth classic, but was lost by the time of the Han Dynasty.

I. *History of Confucianism in Korea*[14]

TODAY, LESS THAN 1% of South Koreans practice Confucianism, which is all but dead as a functioning religion even in the rest of the world.

It is difficult to get an accurate figure of how many people practice Confucianism. Some statistics show that less than 10 million people follow Confucianism, while others show that there are nearly 350 million. This extreme disparity is due to the way in which these figures are reported.

However, one source mentions that there are 6,111,056 people practicing Confucianism, which is 0.09% of the world's population.

Another source mentions that there are 394 million practitioners of what one website calls Chinese traditional religion, which may include Confucianism. It's also worth noting that while many people in China and other Asian countries may not claim to be "Confucianists," the values and relationships of the Confucian ethic are maintained.

Confucius and his teachings have been practically transmitted in their culture and way of thinking. He is simply part of them. It's difficult to provide an exact percentage, but it seems that a small percentage of the world's population, likely less than 1%, practices Confucianism.

Confucianism in South Korea is often seen as a cultural and ethical framework rather than a distinct religious identity. Therefore, much of the country's culture is Confucianism in philosophy.

It is important to remember that Confucianism's philosophy is far older than Confucius himself. The philosophy behind Confucianism came to Korea in 1122 B.C. by its founder, Keuinja (Viscount of the Shang Dynasty in China). He brought two works, Sijun and Sojun, which were prototypes of the works that now bear those names.

In 550 B.C. Korea received the works that he had edited but Confucianism was not accepted as a religion until the 2nd century A.D.

In A.D. 147, the King of the Shilla dynasty put to death several scholars. Since Buddhism was not formally accepted until A.D. 525, these scholars must have been Confucian philosophers.

During the Shilla Dynasty, the Confucian custom of wearing mourning garments for three years for the death of a parent was introduced. Confucianism continued to make greater influence and in A.D. 700, Sul Chong, a famous Confucian scholar, imported pictures of Confucius from China.

In A.D. 953, the Koryo Dynasty introduced Confucian examinations, a promotional system for filling government positions. It was adopted in the late 10th century and became extremely important, and Koreans began traveling to China to study Confucianism.

It introduced a system of education, ceremony, and civil administration. Once the religion was adopted, it was encouraged and taught all over the country. The values, thoughts, customs, and habits that were derived from the religion were planted in the followers' minds.

In 1441, King Sejong invented the Korean alphabet. Many Confucian books were printed in this text and became available to the masses. By 1805, Confucianism had reached its peak of popularity. In 1876, Korea opened up to the outside world and soon realized that a knowledge of the classic Confucian writings was not the best preparation for public service.

In 1895 (Kapo Nyun), the great examinations were abolished, and Confucianism began to lose its influence as a religion.

Influence of Confucianism in Korea

TEMPLE SACRIFICES ARE still practiced in Korea though Confucianism itself is all but dead. Confucianism has no real priestly system and in early Korea, any scholar could officiate the sacrifices, which were largely uncooked.

Ancestral Worship is considered one of the most vital influences of ancient Confucianism and is a major part of Korean culture today. Even the grave itself is chosen with meticulous detail according to rules and laws derived from Confucian philosophy.

The greatest worship days were the first and third anniversary of the deceased when family members gathered for mourning. One of the greatest debates in Korea is whether or not it is right for a Christian to participate in this worship, but its roots and its activity make it an unbiblical act.

Influence on Modern Society

TODAY, LESS THAN 1% of South Koreans practice Confucianism. However, much of the country's culture and philosophy are based on Confucianism.

When Confucianism first entered Korea, it was not completely accepted. However, it was adopted in the late 10th century and became extremely important. It brought a system of education, ceremony, and civil administration.

Once the religion was adopted, it was encouraged and taught all over the country. The values, thoughts, customs, and habits that were derived from the religion were planted in the followers' minds.

It is said that Confucianism, through its effects on South Korea, helped modernize the country. In actuality, it probably slowed progress since it was a major contributor to the "Hermit Kingdom" mentality that existed for many years.

However, although the religion had a great impact, today, in South Korea, it and its followers dwindle compared to other main religions, such as Christianity and Buddhism.

Teachings and Beliefs

CONFUCIANISM TEACHES that there is a natural social order to society which can best be explained through the Five Relationships:

- Ruler to the ruled.
- Father to the son.
- Older brother to the younger brother.
- Husband to the wife.
- Friend to friend.

In these relationships, the second role is considered subordinate to the first. It was taught that if everyone knew his place in society, then order would prevail.

Several concepts needed to be practiced to achieve an ordered society:

- ***Jen*** - Human kindness should be shown towards one another.

- ***Li*** - Proper etiquette should always be used, and one should strive to achieve perfect virtue.

- ***Filial Piety*** - One should respect their elders.

Biblical Examination of Confucianism

THE ETHICAL SYSTEM taught by Confucius has much to commend, for virtue is something to desire highly. However, the ethical philosophy Confucius espoused was one of self-effort, leaving no room or need for God.

Thus, even in those areas where we would tend to agree, there are glaring imbalances of application. Notice this in the "Five Relationships":

- **Ruler to the ruled** - Although there is a sense in which this is biblical (see Eph 6:5-6; 1 Tim 6:1-2), Confucianism puts the master in such a position that he is practically unaccountable to anyone for his actions. This is contrary to Colossians 4:1 and Ephesians 6:9.

Colossians 4:1 Masters, give unto your servants that which is just and equal; knowing that ye also have a Master in heaven.

Ephesians 6:9 And, ye masters, do the same things unto them, forbearing threatening: knowing that your Master also is in heaven; neither is there respect of persons with him.

- **Father to son**—Again, this is a biblical principle as well (Ephesians 6:1; Colossians 3:20). However, in a Confucianist society, it is often taken to an extreme. In many Asian cultures, the Father (and sometimes the mother) retains absolute authority, not only during a child's growth and maturity but often even after marriage. This is another example of an improperly applied principle that is actually a biblical truth.

Genesis 2:23-25 And Adam said, This is now bone of my bones, and flesh of my flesh: she shall be called Woman, because she was taken out of Man. 24 Therefore shall a man leave his father and his mother, and shall cleave unto his wife: and they shall be one flesh. 25 And they were both naked, the man and his wife, and were not ashamed.

- **Older brother to younger brother** - According to the Scriptures, the older brother received a larger inheritance (Genesis 25:31-34; Deuteronomy 21:15-17). It was understood that he would someday become the head of the clan. This is also expressed within the framework of a Confucianist society. However, the application of this relationship is not so accurately defined. Thus it is difficult to see any real difference between the biblical view and the Confucianist view. However, as in the other relationships as well, the "higher" one is almost above accountability in their treatment of the "lower" one.

- ***Husband to wife*** - In Confucianism, the wife is completely subservient to the husband. Again, some would see this as a biblical principle as well.

However, in Confucianism, this is taken to an incredible extreme:

- The wife is something owned and has no will of her own. She has and must express, only the will of the husband.

- The wife has no rights. She is found to be of value only in her relationship with her husband.

- The husband is never wrong. When in doubt see rule #1!

However, several factors must be considered as we examine this from a biblical perspective:

- In a marriage relationship, the wife voluntarily submits to the husband's leadership. (Genesis 24:58; Ephesians 5:22-23)

- The husband may not mistreat his wife in any way. (Ephesians 5:25-31)

- ***Friend to friend*** - In Confucianist societies, friendship is a very well-defined term. Friends must be of the same social status and age. This is taken to the extreme that one child may not be the friend of another child although they may be only one year apart.[15] Nowadays, this distinction is not so pronounced in adults.

Again, this is an influence based on Confucianism. It is not necessarily wrong within itself, but it does prevent many people from understanding how Jesus can be our "friend" (John 15:13-15)

Confucianism is a self-centered philosophy that teaches man can do it himself. Christianity teaches that man cannot save himself, but is in desperate need of a savior. (Romans 3:10-23)

Confucius also hinted that human nature is good. Later Confucian teachers developed this thought, which became a cardinal belief of Confucianism.

The Bible, on the other hand, teaches that man is sinful and, when left to himself, is completely incapable of performing ultimate good.

> ***Romans 3:10-12*** *As it is written, There is none righteous, no, not one:* ***11*** *There is none that understandeth, there is none that seeketh after God.* ***12*** *They are all gone out of the way, they are together become unprofitable; there is none that doeth good, no, not one.*

It must be remembered that Confucius taught an ethical philosophy that later germinated into a popular religion, though Confucius had no idea that his teachings would become the state religion in China.

Nevertheless, Confucianism as a religious system is opposed to the teachings of Christianity and must be completely rejected by Christians.

S hamanism has been called a system of beliefs that supposedly maximizes human abilities of mind and spirit for healing and problem-solving.

The word "shamanism," comes from a Siberian tribal word for its practitioners, "shaman". Shamans are said to have the ability to visit hidden worlds otherwise mainly known through myth, dreams, and near-death experiences.

Traditional shamanism is where the shaman functions as a healer, spiritual leader, and mediator between the spirits and people[1].

Shamanistic psychotherapy, a form of modern psychology, employs shamanistic techniques to produce *"psycho-spiritual integration,"* explore the unconscious, contact one's *"higher self,"* and so on.

Shamanistic medicine includes the application of animistic and various ancient witchcraft techniques to health care. It may involve either shamanism itself as a means to health and enlightenment (shaman initiation and following the shaman's "life path"), or the use of specific shamanistic techniques in conjunction with a particular health program (e.g., visualization, altered states of consciousness, dreams, or the use of "power animals," which are spirits that appear in the form of animals, birds, or other creatures).

Modern Shamanism claims to bring about some form of personal power, spiritual enlightenment, or physical healing to its adherents. When considered from this light, psychic surgeons, New Age mediums, channelers, and Eastern gurus are "spiritual cousins" of the Shamanists.

Other modern forms go by the names - Spiritism, spirit possession, kundalini arousal, psychic healing, and various occult practices.

History of Shamanism

SHAMANISM'S FOUNDER is unknown. It has existed in some form or practice in almost every culture and society throughout history. In South Korea, Shamanism is one of the oldest religions in the country.

---

1.   http://www.inplainsite.org/html/channelling.html

It has existed as a somewhat folksy superstition but entered mainstream religion as an organized religion in the 1970s. Less than one percent of the Korean population holds to a shamanistic system of beliefs. However, it is not uncommon for Koreans to consult a shaman for guidance before making an important decision.

Beliefs

SHAMANISM IS DIFFICULT to define because its beliefs and practices are so entwined with its cultural setting. There is no one major dogma, set ritual, or central authority. It has been described as one of the most diverse of all pagan religions.

Shamanism is the worshiping of the spirits of nature. It is based on the belief that human beings not only possess a spirit but that they are also connected to the spirits that reside in objects of nature.

Similar to Hinduism, the number of spirits (gods) that can be worshipped is in the thousands. The followers worship thousands of spirits and demons that dwell in everyday objects in the natural world (similar to pantheism.)

In Shamanism, the living is responsible for solving "conflicts" or "tension" between spirits.

One seemingly consistent thread is the desire for a "vision-quest" or altered state of consciousness. To achieve this, some Shamans employ the use of hallucinogenic drugs. Others, however, frown on this practice.

Biblical Warnings Against Shamanism

IT SHOULD BE SAID THAT using shamanistic techniques and methods in any given program (e.g., visualization, altered states of consciousness, sensory manipulation, dream work) is not equivalent to following the shamanistic path.

Shamanistic methods can be used independently in various ways; they may or may not introduce one to pursuing the path of the shaman. Shamanism also bears a significant relationship to modern cultism. In the last generation, the revival of new American cults and religions illustrates several shamanistic motifs.

Shamanism leads to spirit possession and other forms of occult bondage. For example, in shamanistic healing the acquiring of true health demands both the practitioner and patient to be "energized" by his or her "power animal," or spirit guide.

Possession by one or more spirits for empowerment, enlightenment, personal health maintenance, and healing abilities is necessary and encouraged.

Temporary insanity, demon possession, and tremendous physical suffering are some of the effects. Those treated with shamanistic techniques or methods may become converted to the occult.

All fortune-telling, sorcery, forms of astrology, omens, charms, spells, or mediums are strictly prohibited by God.

> ***Deuteronomy 18:10-12*** *There shall not be found among you any one that maketh his son or his daughter to pass through the fire, or that useth divination, or an observer of times, or an enchanter, or a witch,* ***11*** *Or a charmer, or a consulter with familiar spirits, or a wizard, or a necromancer.* ***12*** *For all that do these things are an abomination unto the LORD: and because of these abominations the LORD thy God doth drive them out from before thee.*

The Scriptures state that such use leads to defilement and judgment.

> ***Leviticus 19:31*** *Regard not them that have familiar spirits, neither seek after wizards, to be defiled by them: I am the LORD your God.*

God also gives very strict warnings concerning those who do not heed his commands.

> ***Leviticus 20:6*** *And the soul that turneth after such as have familiar spirits, and after wizards, to go a whoring after them, I will even set my face against that soul, and will cut him off from among his people.*

Taoism

Taoism is a spiritual practice over 2,500 years old which is similar to Zen Buddhism in some ways. The main texts of Taoism are the "Tao-te Ching" (The Book of the Way and Its Power) by Lao Tzu and "Inner Chapters" by Chuang Tzu.

There are two existing forms of Taoism today – a "Philosophical-Spiritual Taoism" and a more traditional form that incorporates different modes of divination and even alchemy.

Beliefs

THE TAOIST IDEA OF "God" is a supreme being or ultimate truth that can not be expressed by words or understood conceptually. It is referred to as simply "Tao" or "the Way". However, Taoists seldom refer to God.

Taoists believe that all matter is a manifestation of "Tao", which makes it a pantheistic philosophy. As a concept, Taoists do not hold the position of good against evil; rather they see the interdependence of all dualities.

So when one labels something as good, one automatically creates evil. That is, all concepts necessarily are based on one aspect versus another; if a concept were to have only one aspect, it would be nonsensical.

All actions are thought to contain some aspect of good and evil. This is represented in the t'ai chi, more commonly referred to as the yin-yang symbol. Taoists believe that nature is a continual balance between yin and yang and that any attempt to go toward one extreme or the other will be ineffective, self-defeating, and short-lived.

Taoists do not practice or believe in any "salvation doctrine" because they do not believe there is anything to be saved from! Belief in salvation would lead to belief in damnation in the same manner as belief in good leads to belief in evil.

They do not accept the duality of salvation versus damnation but believe that living simply in harmony with Te and Tao and not excessively pursuing materialism will lead to a joyful life.

Biblical Analysis

AS WITH ANY PHILOSOPHY, without Christ, all hope is lost. For the Taoist, this is only complicated by the belief that there is no need for salvation in the first place. Thus, even if they acknowledged the existence of Christ, they would not see a need to accept him as Savior.

The Tao concept of many elements that are contrary to one another, i.e. male/female, positive/negative, light/darkness, active/passive, and life/death is also philosophically faulty.

How does a Taoist know that his philosophy is not some misguided "yin" in need of the "yang" or truth? Obviously, the answer is simply that he must place his faith in "Taoism" as being true.

This very act goes against the principles of Taoism which states that **everything** is a balance of the true and false! But take note of the words of Scripture:

> ***John 14:6*** *Jesus saith unto him, I am the way, the truth, and the life: no man cometh unto the Father, but by me.*

> ***John 8:32*** *And ye shall know the truth, and the truth shall make you free.*

> ***Acts 17:23-24*** *For as I passed by, and beheld your devotions, I found an altar with this inscription, TO THE UNKNOWN GOD. Whom therefore ye ignorantly worship, him declare I unto you. **24** God that made the world and all things therein, seeing that he is Lord of heaven and earth, dwelleth not in temples made with hands;*

Taoists believe that God is completely inexpressible. Then how does the Taoist express "Tao" as "stillness, placidity, silence, etc.? These are words that are descriptive of **mindlessness**. However, we are to love God with all our minds.

> ***Matthew 22:37*** *Jesus said unto him, Thou shalt love the Lord thy God with all thy heart, and with all thy soul, and with all thy mind.*

"An idle mind is the Devil's workshop" *Anonymous*

The Taoist believes in a pantheistic view of God, while the Scriptures teach that God is Creator and therefore outside of His creation (Gen 1:1, etc.)

Genesis 1:1 *In the beginning God created the heaven and the earth.*

Hinduism

Hinduism is actually a regional/people group descriptive name. It is the name of the inhabitants and the religion of the Indus River region. The inhabitants were called Hindus and their religion was called Hinduism.

Yet Hinduism today covers a diverse number of beliefs, with a few unifying themes. Hindus are found mainly in the nation of India, where over 90% of Hindus live.

There are also large populations of Hindus in Nepal, Mauritius, Fiji, Guyana, Suriname, Bangladesh, Malaysia, Trinidad and Tabago, and Bhutan.

The latest estimates suggest that the population of Hindus is around 1.15 billion individuals, making it one of the largest religious groups in the world. This number is constantly changing due to various factors such as birth rates, death rates, and conversions.

History of Hinduism

THE HISTORY OF HINDUISM comes from the Aryan peoples[16] who moved to the Indus Valley in northwestern India around 1500 B.C. Over the next few centuries, they conquered the entire subcontinent of India. They brought with them an Aryan religion of what was then in Iran, somewhat similar to Zoroastrianism.[17]

Different "ways" have developed over the history of Hinduism, Vedic Hinduism being the oldest, and then the ascetic and mystical way known as Vedantic Hinduism, and more recently the way of devotion, or Bhakti.

Hinduism has flourished in the Western world through various New Age philosophies and fads such as Yoga, Transcendental Mediation[18], and various other New Age religions (Bahaism, Divine Light Mission, Krishna Consciousness, Vedanta Society, etc.)

Hindu Holy Books

THE OLDEST AND MOST revered holy writings are the Vedas[19], consisting of four books or more correctly—collections. They are:

- The Rig Veda
- Sama Veda
- Yajur Veda
- Atharva Veda

These are sacrificial hymns, chants, rituals, and explanations.

In addition to the Vedas, numerous other writings have been added through the years. These include:

- *Upanishads*—Common topics are: states of consciousness, dreams, meditations, self-realization (that you are divine), and the unity of all things.

- *Darshanas*—Six major schools or Philosophical systems and teachings developed out of the Vedas: Nyaga, Mimamsa, Vaiseshika, Yoga, Samkhya, and Vendata.

- *The Puranas*—myths and stories of the more recent gods of India.

- *The Tantras* - a distinct branch of the devotion movement with an emphasis on the power of the divine feminine or goddess.

- *Ramayana*—an account of the noble king, Ram, and his act of rescuing his wife, Sita, who was abducted. He does this with the help of Hanuman, the monkey god.

- *Mahabharata*—an account of the war between two families, the Pandavas and the Kauravas. The Mahabharata includes the text of the Bhagavad Gita, perhaps the most popular of all Hindu texts.

Beliefs

REINCARNATION. Man is trapped in a nearly endless series of rebirths (samsara). All creatures are in the struggle to ascend the ladder of rebirths through the lower forms of life up to human life, through the lower castes, to the highest caste of the Brahmins, finally achieving after thousands of reincarnations- release (moksha) or liberation.

Karma. Karma is believed to be the law that entraps and keeps a soul in samsara, the long process of rebirth after rebirth. There are different types of karma:

- *Sanchita*—the karma with which one is born that has come from previous lives.

- *Kriyaman*—the karma of your present life's actions.

- *Agama*—karma produced by our thoughts and plans for our life.

- *Prarandha*—and the karma that is determined to be in force for this present life

There is also the karma of your people and culture. Karma is used to explain evil in that if something terrible happens to a person with no seeming connection to their direct actions, it is assumed that the law of karma is bringing to bear the bad fruit of past actions.

Dharma. This means religion or duty. One knows one's duty in society by determining one's caste placement and stage of life.

Caste. The law of karma determines your placement in society, in one of four major castes: Brahmins (priests), Kshatriyas (warriors and rulers), Vaishyas (merchants), and Shudras (workers). The three higher castes are termed 'twice-born' and are given full participation in society.

The Shudra caste exists to do the manual labor of the society and is considered impure to the higher castes. Outcastes or untouchables have little or no standing in society and do work that renders them unclean.

Though the caste system is formally abolished in India, it is still conceptually essential in the Hindu concept of dharma, karma, and reincarnation.

Hindu view of Christ

HINDUISM DOES NOT REFER to Jesus in its scriptures, and He plays no role in any of the classical Hindu mythology. Nevertheless, due to the contact with Christianity, some Hindu thinkers have found a place for Jesus in their view.

These considerations have taken the form of two particularly noteworthy ideas:

The first one is that Jesus was one of the incarnations (avatars) of God. Most Hindus believe that God, specifically Vishnu, took on human or animal forms at various times to perform certain feats that would preserve true Hindu teaching (the dharma).

In this context, then, it has been argued that Jesus, along with Rama, Krishna, and others, was just one more divine self-embodiment. Whereas Christians generally believe that Jesus was the only incarnation of God, this view would hold that he was an incarnation, just not the only one.

The second way of trying to incorporate Jesus into Hinduism is to ***claim that Jesus learned the teachings that he later proclaimed in India***. According to this notion, Jesus spent his so-called "silent years" between ages twelve and thirty at the feet of Hindu masters in India, and it is their teaching that he then proclaimed during his ministry.

However, the teachings of Christ share little to nothing in common with the teachings of Hinduism.

Salvation. In Hinduism, salvation is most frequently referred to as "moksha," which means most literally "release." One is saved, not from sin, but from one's own existence.

The point of moksha is to be released from the cycle of reincarnation and to attain a state of bliss in union with God.

Hinduism has traditionally recognized three main paths of salvation:

- ***The "way of works"***—an attempt to purify the soul by the meticulous observance of all the laws and obligations of the Hindu scriptures.

- ***The "way of knowledge"*** —the total renunciation of all one's life and to seek salvation in a mystical realization of identity with God.

- ***The "way of devotion (bhakti)"*** - Total commitment to the worship of a particular god or goddess who will then take care of one's karma problems and usher him into fellowship with him when he dies.

The result will be a state of bliss in union with God (sometimes conceived of as identity with God). Heaven, as Christians think of it, would not be the goal since one would still be sent from heaven back to further physical life.

God. It is estimated that there are over 300 million gods in Hinduism. One cannot help but be stricken with shock and awe, even terror at the untold thousands of idols and idolatrous temples in Hindu nations. It is almost beyond belief.

Many Hindus believe that the universe is simply an illusion and "God" is an impersonal oneness. In other words, everything is a part of the force (monism). Nothing is distinct and separate from anything else.

Man extends from and is one with Brahman. All is one, all is God—and that means that we are God. According to Hinduism, humanity's primary problem is that we have forgotten we are divine. The consequence is that we are subject to the Law of Karma, the moral equivalent to the natural law of cause and effect.

Biblical Analysis

THE SCRIPTURES CLEARLY warn against any idolatrous practices:

Exodus 20:3-6 Thou shalt have no other gods before me. 4 Thou shalt not make unto thee any graven image, or any likeness of any thing that is in heaven above, or that is in the earth beneath, or that is in the water under the earth: 5 Thou shalt not bow down thyself to them, nor serve them: for I the LORD thy God am a jealous God, visiting the iniquity of the fathers upon the children unto the third and fourth generation of them that hate me; 6 And shewing mercy unto thousands of them that love me, and keep my commandments.

Exodus 20:23 Ye shall not make with me gods of silver, neither shall ye make unto you gods of gold.

Exodus 23:13 *And in all things that I have said unto you be circumspect: and make no mention of the name of other gods, neither let it be heard out of thy mouth.*

Deuteronomy 4:16-18 *Lest ye corrupt yourselves, and make you a graven image, the similitude of any figure, the likeness of male or female,* ***17*** *The likeness of any beast that is on the earth, the likeness of any winged fowl that flieth in the air,* ***18*** *The likeness of any thing that creepeth on the ground, the likeness of any fish that is in the waters beneath the earth:*

Romans 1:23 *And changed the glory of the uncorruptible God into an image made like to corruptible man, and to birds, and fourfooted beasts, and creeping things.*

Hinduism believes in reincarnation. However, the Scriptures teach that death is followed by judgment.

Hebrews 9:27 *And as it is appointed unto men once to die, but after this the judgment:*

Hindus may accept Christ as another one of their gods; however, biblically speaking, there is only one God.

1 Timothy 2:5 *For there is one God, and one mediator between God and men, the man Christ Jesus;*

Mark 12:32 *And the scribe said unto him, Well, Master, thou hast said the truth: for there is one God; and there is none other but he:*

Deuteronomy 4:39 *Know therefore this day, and consider it in thine heart, that the LORD he is God in heaven above, and upon the earth beneath: there is none else.*

Isaiah 44:8 *Fear ye not, neither be afraid: have not I told thee from that time, and have declared it? ye are even my witnesses. Is there a God beside me? yea, there is no God; I know not any.*

One of the problems with Hinduism is that it teaches Monistic Pantheism (All is One and All is God). This leads to a God who is impersonal, unknowing, and unknowable.

The Indian philosopher Shankara (8th century) described this worldview as a seamless garment in which absolutely everything is Brahman (God). The material universe may appear to exist, but it is only Maya (illusion).

The problem is that the material universe has a way of making its presence known in very "concrete" ways. As one contemporary Indian philosopher put it, "Even in India, we look both ways before we cross the street".

If "All is One and all is God", then ethics is also an illusion (Maya). Swami Vivekananda (1863-1902) stated, "Really, good and evil are one and the same." Theoretically, once you are "enlightened" you have transcended good and evil. All actions, even evil ones, are "enlightened" ones.

A Biblical worldview (the personal, creator God being separate from His creation) is far more testable and consistent with reality. In Romans 2, the Apostle Paul states that this personal, moral God of creation, in creating man in His own image, placed a moral conscience within the heart of each human being.

Thus, people intuitively "know" what is right and wrong. This can be demonstrated anthropologically by investigating human cultures down through time.

History of Islam

The term "Islam" means "submission" to the will of God, and the person who submits is called a "Muslim."

Muhammad, who was born in AD 570, is the founder of Islam. During his youth, he often retreated to a cave at the summit of Mount Hira just outside of Mecca.

At age 40, he claimed to begin receiving revelations from a spirit being he believed was the angel Gabriel. These later were recorded and became the Qur'an, Islam's holy book. (note the warning of Galatians 1:8-9).

> **Galatians 1:8-9** *But though we, or an angel from heaven, preach any other gospel unto you than that which we have preached unto you, let him be accursed.* **9** *As we said before, so say I now again, If any man preach any other gospel unto you than that ye have received, let him be accursed.*

Mohammed began proselytizing by preaching a message of strict Monotheism and judgment. He also began strongly condemning the social evils of his day.

His message appealed to the economically poor who were being mistreated and oppressed by the wealthy. Most of his initial followers came from this group.

The elite class living in Mecca felt threatened by his message and persecuted Muhammad and his followers.

After the death of his wife and uncle, he eventually left Mecca on a journey known to Muslims as the Hijra, or "journey (A.D. 622). This event marks the beginning of the Islamic calendar.

It is also important to know that this migration is prompted by persecution in Mecca and represents a significant turning point in Islamic history.

He settled in the area of Yathrib (now known as Medina) with his followers and became the leader of the first Muslim community.

Six years of continuous war between Muslim and Meccan forces finally led to a bloodless Muslim victory and conquest of Mecca. The Muslims subsequently removed everything they considered idolatrous from the Kaaba. [20] Most of the townspeople accepted Islam.

In March 632, Muhammad led the pilgrimage known as the Hajj. On returning to Medina, he fell ill and died after a few days, on June 8, 632.

Muhammad is considered the last prophet in a line that includes figures like Adam, Noah, Abraham, Moses, and Jesus.

Under those who assumed authority after his death, the Islamic empire expanded into Palestine, Syria, Mesopotamia, Persia, Egypt, North Africa, southern Spain, and Asia Minor.

Later conquests, commercial contact between Muslims and non-Muslims, and missionary activity spread Islam over much of the Eastern Hemisphere, including China and Southeast Asia.

Today, Islam is the second-largest religion in the world, with over 1.8 billion adherents. It is diverse, with various sects and interpretations, the largest being Sunni and Shia Islam. Islam continues to play a crucial role in the cultural, social, and political life of many countries across the globe.

Six Articles of Faith in Islam

THE SIX ARTICLES OF Faith in Islam are fundamental beliefs that every Muslim is expected to hold. These articles form the core of a Muslim's faith and understanding of their religion.

There is no God but Allah. There are three large monotheistic religions in the world – Islam, Judaism, and Christianity. They all proclaim to have the correct form of worship to the same God. However, the Islamic definition of God in his character and will is not the God of Christianity or Judaism.

In the Qur'an, Allah is a distant spiritual being, but God is a Father to His children. Allah does not love wrongdoers, but God commends His love toward us in that while we were still sinners, Christ died for us.

Muslims do not believe in one God eternally existing in three persons—the Father, the Son, and the Holy Spirit. The doctrine of the Trinity for them appears to be an abomination. Islam does not believe in the divinity of Christ. But what does the Bible teach concerning this?

1 John 4:2-3 Hereby know ye the Spirit of God: Every spirit that confesseth that Jesus Christ is come in the flesh is of God: 3 And every spirit that confesseth not that Jesus Christ is come in the flesh is not of God: and this is that spirit of antichrist, whereof ye have heard that it should come; and even now already is it in the world.

2 John 1:7 For many deceivers are entered into the world, who confess not that Jesus Christ is come in the flesh. This is a deceiver and an antichrist.

The second Article of Faith is the belief in a hierarchy of angels, of which the archangel Gabriel is the highest. Each Muslim is assigned two angels, one to record his good deeds and the other to record his bad deeds. At the bottom of the angelic hierarchy is the jinn, from which we get the word "genie". They are a Muslim version of demons.

In Islamic culture, a "genie" (or "jinni" in Arabic, plural "jinn") is a supernatural being created by Allah from smokeless, scorching fire. They are part of the unseen world and have qualities that are both similar to and distinct from humans and angels. Jinn generally exist in a realm that is invisible to humans but can sometimes make themselves visible or influence the physical world. Jinn are believed to interact with humans in various ways. They can inspire thoughts, appear in dreams, or even possess individuals.

The third Article of Faith is the belief in 104 holy books, with the Koran as the final revelation. Islam accepts the Law of Moses, the Psalms, and, surprisingly, the Gospels, but believes the Bible is badly flawed and cannot be trusted.

The fourth is belief in the prophets. According to the Qur'an, God has sent a prophet to every nation to preach the message that there is only one God.

124,000 prophets have been sent, most of them unknown, but some of them are biblical characters, including Adam, Noah (Nuh), Abraham (Ibrahim), Moses (Musa), David (Dawud), and Jesus (Isa). Mohammed, though, is the prophet for all times, the "Seal of the Prophets."

The fifth Article of Faith is the belief in predestination (Qadar). All things, both good and evil, are the direct result of the will of Allah. Islam is a very fatalistic religion.

The sixth Article of Faith is the Day of Judgment. Those whose good deeds outweigh their bad will be rewarded with Paradise; those whose bad deeds outweigh their good will be judged to hell. Thus, Islam is a religion of human works. (note Eph 2:8-9)

> ***Ephesians 2:8-9*** *For by grace are ye saved through faith; and that not of yourselves: it is the gift of God:* ***9*** *Not of works, lest any man should boast.*

Five Pillars of Islam

THE FIVE PILLARS OF Islam are five core beliefs and practices that every Muslim must keep. They form the foundation of a Muslim's faith and actions and are essential to the practice of Islam.

1. ***Shahada (Faith)*** - Reciting the creed, "There is no God but Allah, and Mohammed is his messenger." This declaration affirms the monotheistic belief in Allah and the acceptance of Muhammad as His final prophet.
2. ***Salah (Prayer)*** - 17 cycles of prayer, spread out over five times of prayer each day. Each prayer involves specific physical postures and recitations from the Quran. They must wash in a prescribed manner before they kneel and face toward Mecca.
3. ***Zakat (Almsgiving)*** - the practice of giving a fixed portion of one's wealth (typically 2.5% of accumulated wealth) to those in need, including the poor, orphans, and widows. Zakat purifies wealth by redistributing it and ensuring that the community's needs are met, promoting social justice and reducing economic disparities.
4. ***Sawm (Fasting during Ramadan)*** - During daylight hours, Muslims must forego food, water, and physical relations. Children, the elderly, the sick, travelers, pregnant or nursing women, and those who face health risks are exempt from fasting, though they may need to make up the fast later or provide charity.
5. Hajj (Pilgrimage to Mecca) - Every Muslim who is physically and financially able must perform the Hajj pilgrimage at least once in their lifetime. The pilgrimage takes place annually during the Islamic month

of Dhu al-Hijjah. Hajj involves a series of specific rituals, including the Tawaf (circumambulating the Kaaba), Sa'i (walking between the hills of Safa and Marwah), standing at Arafat, and the symbolic stoning of the devil.Hajj commemorates the trials of Prophet Ibrahim (Abraham) and his family.

Muslim Beliefs Versus The Bible

MUSLIM SALVATION IS dependent upon works which is in contrast to the Scriptural basis of salvation by faith. In addition, Islam denies the basic tenets of the orthodox Christian faith. Below is a table showing quotes from the Quran and the counter-argument from the Bible.

Islamic Beliefs	Christianity

God has no Son: Surah 19:88-93, "To say that God has a son is assuredly a disastrous thing, whereby the heavens are almost torn, the earth split asunder, and the mountains fall in ruin. God has no son but everyone has to come to God as a slave."

The Bible clearly teaches that Jesus is God's Only Begotten Son. John 1:18; John 1:14, John 3:16-18; 1 John 4:9

God is not a Trinity: Surah 4:48, 171, "Allah forgiveth not that partners should be set up with Him... Say not "Trinity": desist: it will be better for you: for Allah is one Allah: Glory be to Him: (far exalted is He) above having a son. To Him belong all things in the heavens and on earth. And enough is Allah as a Disposer of affairs." Surah 5:73 "They do blaspheme who say: Allah is one of three in a Trinity: for there is no god except One Allah. If they desist not from their word (of blasphemy), verily a grievous penalty will befall the blasphemers among them.

There are ample texts speaking of the Trinity. John 10:30-33, John 20:28; Isa 9:6, Matthew 1:23; Romans 9:5; Philippians 2:6; 1 Timothy 3:16; Titus 2:13; Hebrews 1:8-13; 1 John 5:7, 1 John 5:20

Jesus was not God: Surah 3:59 "Verily, the likeness of Isa (Jesus) before Allah is the likeness of Adam. He created him of dust, then (He) said to him: 'Be!'- and he was."

Jesus was not crucified: Surah 4:157 "That they said (in boast), "We killed Christ Jesus the son of Mary, the Messenger of Allah";- *but they killed him not, nor crucified him,* but so it was made to appear to them, and those who differ therein are full of doubts, with no (certain) knowledge, but only conjecture to follow, for of a surety they killed him not."

This is the central message of the New Testament. Matthew 26:2; 27:22-44; 28:5; Mark 15:15-32; 16:6; Luke 23:23, 33; 24:7, 20; John 19:16-41; Acts 2:23, 36; 4:10; Romans 6:6; 1 Corinthians 1:13, 23; 2:2, 8; 2 Corinthians 13:4; Galatians 2:20; 3:1; 5:24; 6:14; Revelation 11:8

Blood is unimportant to Allah. Surah 22:34-37, ...We made animals subject to you, that ye may be

Again, without the blood, there is no cleansing of sin. Matthew 26:28; Mark

grateful. *It is not their meat nor their blood, that reaches Allah: it is your piety that reaches Him*: He has thus made them subject to you, that ye may glorify Allah for His Guidance to you and proclaim the good news to all who do right."

<u>There is no atonement for sin in Jesus:</u> Surah 4:171 "O People of the Scripture (Christians)! Do not exaggerate in your religion nor utter aught concerning Allah, save the truth. The *Messiah, Jesus son of Mary, was only a messenger of Allah,* and His word, which He conveyed unto Mary, and a spirit from him. So believe in Allah and His messengers, and say not 'Three'—Cease!" Surah 5:75, "*Christ the son of Mary was no more than a messenger*; many were the messengers that passed away before him. ... See how Allah doth make His signs clear to them; yet see in what ways they are deluded away from the truth!"

14:24; Luke 11:50, 51; 22:20; John 6:53, 54, 55, 56; 19:34; Acts 20:28; Romans 3:25; 5:9; 1 Corinthians 10:16; 11:25, 27; Galatians 1:16; Ephesians 1:7; 2:13; etc.

There is salvation *only* in Jesus. Matthew 9:2, 5, 6; 12:31, 32; 18:21, 35; Mark 2:5, 7, 9, 10; 4:12; 11:25, 26; Luke 5:20, 21, 23, 24; 6:37; 7:47, 48, 49; 11:4; 12:10; 17:3, 4; 23:34; Acts 5:31; 8:22; 13:38; 26:18; Romans 4:7; 2 Corinthians 2:7, 10; 12:13; Ephesians 1:7; Colossians 1:14; 2:13; James 5:15; 1 John 1:9; 2:12

Additional Observations

IN ARAB COUNTRIES, women usually hold a very low position and are looked down on, regarded as those that tempt men to sin. Islam permits up to 4 wives.

Islam now is the major religion of the Arab countries and has also made inroads in Africa, Southeast Asia, Europe, and even the United States.

Those who do not follow Islam are considered infidels. Sometimes those who practice Islam in another group, sect, or faction would also be considered an infidel.

Islam is a violent religion. It is written in Surah 47:4 - *When you meet (in El Jihad), those who disbelieve, smite at their necks till you have killed and wounded many of them.* Surah 9:5 - *Kill the idolaters wheresoever ye shall find them.* Note the difference in the Bible.

Matthew 5:44 But I say unto you, Love your enemies, bless them that curse you, do good to them that hate you, and pray for them which despitefully use you, and persecute you;

Luke 6:27-28 But I say unto you which hear, Love your enemies, do good to them which hate you, 28 Bless them that curse you, and pray for them which despitefully use you.

The Islamic Allah commands death to those who do not convert to Islam, but God demands that their salvation be sought.

Luke 9:56 For the Son of man is not come to destroy men's lives, but to save them. And they went to another village.

The goal of Muslims is world domination through Islam, by whatever means is necessary, and thus have a moral order everywhere. The question arises, is there peace when Islam takes over? The answer is no. There is still killing, terror, and violence.

There are various factions within Islam. Their beliefs differ in some areas, especially politically. Some of its extremists can be extremely militant and violent. As a result, there have even been wars between various Islamic groups.

No religious freedom exists in most countries that practice this religion. They believe once a nation becomes Islamic, it must always remain so. Thus, they believe the land of Israel, which was once under Islamic rule, must revert back to the Muslims. The Jews must be killed, driven out, or converted to Islam.

Judaism is the religion of the Jewish people. Since it is so closely tied to Christianity, it shares many biblical and historical similarities. It is based upon the Old Testament Scriptures and is said to have begun with Abraham (circa 2000 B.C.). However, its modern form really began in the 200s A.D.

Its modern form is based not only on the Old Testament but various other religious writings and traditions. Yet even these traditions revolve around the study and observance of the Old Testament Laws.

When the Temple was destroyed in A.D. 70, sacrifices and the priesthood ended. Instead of being guided by prophets, priests, and kings, the Jewish people turned to rabbis as their authority on matters of law and practice.

There was one kind of Judaism until the eighteenth century, when the Age of Enlightenment swept through Europe. Having said that, as in all religious groups, whether biblical or not, there will be differences in interpretation of practice. In Judaism's case, the Pharisees and Sadducees are an example of this in the New Testament.

The three major branches of Judaism arose:

- ***Orthodox Judaism*** – traditional Judaism with a strong emphasis on tradition and strict observance of the Law of Moses.

- ***Reform Judaism*** - began in Germany at the time of the Enlightenment. It is a humanistic branch that contains many Reform Jews who don't believe in God at all. For them, Judaism is a way of life and culture with a connection to one's ancestors that is about legacy, not faith.

- ***Conservative Judaism*** - a middle-ground branch, seeking moderation between the two extremes of the Orthodox and Reform branches.

An estimated 14,000,000 adherents make it the 11th largest organized religion in the world. It is among the oldest monotheistic religions still in practice today.

Beliefs

THE MOST IMPORTANT of all Jewish beliefs is their belief in a single omniscient, omnipotent, benevolent, transcendent God who created all things. If there is any religious principle that Judaism explicitly affirms and teaches, it is the unity of God.

> **Deuteronomy 6:4** *Hear, O Israel: The LORD our God is one LORD:*

This one all-important principle is one reason so many Jewish people have a hard time understanding Christianity, which they see as a religion of three gods, not one God in three Persons.

It is difficult for Jewish people to place their faith in Jesus as Messiah because it is not considered a Jewish thing to do. In fact, they see "Jewish Christian" as an oxymoron.

Another big reason it is so hard for Jewish people to come to faith in Christ is that many do not see a need for salvation. In their minds, the Jewish people already have a special relationship with God as His chosen people. Jesus is viewed as unnecessary at best, and a false prophet at worst.

Biblical Analysis

IN MANY WAYS, CHRISTIANITY and Judaism are very similar. They both believe in the Jehovah of the Bible, espouse many of the same moral and ethical principles, and have faced untold persecution for their beliefs. The nation of Israel, as well as Christians, are both chosen and preserved by God and hold strong beliefs concerning a coming kingdom.

Problems with Judaism [21]

JUDAISM IS A MAN-MADE religion void of Christ. Although God chose the nation Israel as His vehicle to bring Christ and the Scriptures to mankind, Israel has rejected their own Messiah (Romans 10:1-3, 18-21; Matthew. 26:59, 65-67; 27:20-23).

> **Romans 10:1-3** *Brethren, my heart's desire and prayer to God for Israel is, that they might be saved. 2 For I bear them record that they*

have a zeal of God, but not according to knowledge. 3 For they being ignorant of God's righteousness, and going about to establish their own righteousness, have not submitted themselves unto the righteousness of God.

***Romans 10:18-21** But I say, Have they not heard? Yes verily, their sound went into all the earth, and their words unto the ends of the world. **19** But I say, Did not Israel know? First Moses saith, I will provoke you to jealousy by them that are no people, and by a foolish nation I will anger you. **20** But Esaias is very bold, and saith, I was found of them that sought me not; I was made manifest unto them that asked not after me. **21** But to Israel he saith, All day long I have stretched forth my hands unto a disobedient and gainsaying people.*

***Matthew 26:59** Now the chief priests, and elders, and all the council, sought false witness against Jesus, to put him to death;*

***Matthew 26:65-67** Then the high priest rent his clothes, saying, He hath spoken blasphemy; what further need have we of witnesses? behold, now ye have heard his blasphemy. **66** What think ye? They answered and said, He is guilty of death. **67** Then did they spit in his face, and buffeted him; and others smote him with the palms of their hands,*

***Matthew 27:20-23** But the chief priests and elders persuaded the multitude that they should ask Barabbas, and destroy Jesus. **21** The governor answered and said unto them, Whether of the twain will ye that I release unto you? They said, Barabbas. **22** Pilate saith unto them, What shall I do then with Jesus which is called Christ? They all say unto him, Let him be crucified. **23** And the governor said, Why, what evil hath he done? But they cried out the more, saying, Let him be crucified.*

Even after the resurrection, the Jewish leaders (representatives of the nation itself) rejected Christ (Matthew 28:12-15; Acts 2:36).

Matthew 28:12-15 And when they were assembled with the elders, and had taken counsel, they gave large money unto the soldiers, 13 Saying, Say ye, His disciples came by night, and stole him away while we slept. 14 And if this come to the governor's ears, we will persuade him, and secure you. 15 So they took the money, and did as they were taught: and this saying is commonly reported among the Jews until this day.

Acts 2:36 Therefore let all the house of Israel know assuredly, that God hath made that same Jesus, whom ye have crucified, both Lord and Christ.

Judaism is a manmade attempt to cling to Old Testament patterns that are passed away in Christ Jesus (Hebrews 9).

Hebrews 9:11-14 But Christ being come an high priest of good things to come, by a greater and more perfect tabernacle, not made with hands, that is to say, not of this building; 12 Neither by the blood of goats and calves, but by his own blood he entered in once into the holy place, having obtained eternal redemption for us. 13 For if the blood of bulls and of goats, and the ashes of an heifer sprinkling the unclean, sanctifieth to the purifying of the flesh: 14 How much more shall the blood of Christ, who through the eternal Spirit offered himself without spot to God, purge your conscience from dead works to serve the living God?

Orthodox Jews continue to follow a very vague form of some of the Old Testament laws and practices, largely obscured under a heavy blanket of man-made tradition. But they have no high priest, temple, blood sacrifices, Day of Atonement, altar of sacrifice, ark, and the list goes on!

By rejecting Christ Jesus, they have rejected the great High Priest and the great once-for-all atonement, which was made for sin.

Judaism not only rejects Christ but hates him. One of the statements in the Jewish Talmud teaches that Mary, the Mother of Jesus Christ, was a whore and an adulteress who bore Jesus by a Roman soldier named Pandera. Indeed, Judaism is a Christ-hating religion.

Judaism is a temporary religion. The Bible prophesies that there will come a day when the nation Israel will receive Jesus Christ when He returns from Heaven in power and glory (Zechariah 12:9-10; 13:1,6).

While the Old Testament economy was standing, men were commanded to bring sacrifices, worship in Jerusalem, etc. But now, man can worship God anywhere (John 4:21-24), at any time, through Jesus Christ (John 14:6-9; Acts 4:12; Acts 5:31).

Cults (As Versus World Religions)

Misconceptions Concerning the Danger of Cults

The most dangerous cults are not the Hindus or the Moslems. The most dangerous cults are the ones that look the most like authentic Christianity.

Those who are involved with dissimilar religions know that they are radically different, and they do not pretend to be otherwise.

Those who convert to Christianity from other religions expect radical differences and pose very little problem when taught the truth.

But those who are similar to true Christianity are dangerous on two levels.

First, true believers who lack a solid biblical foundation can easily become swayed by their false teachings. They lack the biblical foundation or discernment to see the differences.

Second, some tend to think that they are not so bad because there is so much we have in common.

A good example of a cult that is extremely similar to authentic Christianity is the Seventh-Day Adventists. They believe that salvation also requires baptism. As a works-based religion, they are a cult. They also believe very many other things that we would agree with, and yet they are a cult.

The Roman Catholic Church claims to be the one true Church, dating back to the beginning, organized by Jesus Christ Himself, with Peter as the first Pope and Vicar of Christ of Earth. However, the Roman Catholic Church was not essentially organized until the time of Constantine about A.D. 314.

For the first three centuries, Christianity was persecuted under various Emperors and powers until Constantine the Great's time. On October 28th, 312 AD, Constantine defeated his rival Maxentius at the battle of the Milvian bridge outside Rome.

According to historical accounts, on the way to this battle, Constantine saw a cross in the sky one afternoon with the words "Hoc vince" (by this conquer), and he adopted the cross as his standard.

Accordingly, Constantine not only accepted Christianity but also made it the religion of the Roman Empire. The result was the Roman Catholic Church, which is a mixture of Christianity and paganism. It was also the beginning of the union of Church and State.

Constantine superimposed Christianity upon these pagan religions, adopting elements of both; thus, by allowing the pagans to continue their heathen customs, he made it easy for them to adopt Christianity. Completely pagan and utterly unbiblical beliefs were given new "Christian" identities. Some clear examples of this are as follows:

- ***The Cult of Isis***, an Egyptian mother-goddess religion, was absorbed into Christianity by replacing Isis with Mary. Many of the titles that were used for Isis, such as "Queen of Heaven," "Mother of God," and "Theotokos" (God-bearer) were attached to Mary.

Many temples to Isis were, in fact, converted into temples dedicated to Mary. The first clear hints of Catholic Mariology occur in the writings of Origen, who lived in Alexandria, Egypt, which happened to be the focal point of Isis worship. (coincidence?)

- *Mithraism*[22] was a religion in the Roman Empire in the 1st through 5th centuries A.D. It was very popular among the Romans, especially among Roman soldiers, and was possibly the religion of several Roman emperors.

One of the key features of Mithraism was a sacrificial meal, which involved eating the flesh and drinking the blood of a bull. Mithras, the god of Mithraism, was "present" in the flesh and blood of the bull, and when consumed, granted salvation to those who partook of the sacrificial meal (theophagy, the eating of one's god). In Catholicism, this is the false teaching of transubstantiation.

Mithraism also had seven "sacraments," making the similarities between it and Roman Catholicism too great to ignore. The Romanization of the Lord's Supper completed the transition to a sacrificial consumption of Jesus Christ, now known as the Catholic Mass / Eucharist.

- Most Roman emperors (and citizens) were *henotheists*.[23] When the Catholic Church absorbed Roman paganism, it simply replaced the pantheon of gods with the saints. Just as the Roman pantheon of gods had a god of love, a god of peace, a god of war, a god of strength, a god of wisdom, etc., so the Catholic Church has a saint who is "in charge" over each of these, and many other categories.

Just as many Roman cities had a god specific to them, the Catholic Church provided "patron saints" for them. While the pretended adoption of Christianity was hailed as a great victory for the Church, it was also, ironically, the beginning of its corruption.

From this date, we can trace all the innumerable errors of the Roman Church—Mariolatry, the mass, purgatory, limbo, the celibacy of the priesthood, adoration and worship of images, indulgences, the infallibility of the Pope, Mary's immaculate conception, and all the other unscriptural errors.

The Roman Church was patronized by the State and subsequently sought temporal powers to rule and govern the State. This was the beginning of the Roman Catholic Church which has lasted until today.

The next great occurrence in the formation of Roman Catholicism came under the leadership of Gregory the Great in A.D. 590. True Catholicism, as we know it today, developed from what we saw in Constantine's time but was not the powerful force it is today until Gregory the Great separated the church from the government in A.D. 590.

To be more exact, Gregory the Great found himself in a situation where the weakness of the government could not, or did not offer protection to the people. This occurred because there was no viable governing authority in Rome. He ended up with incredible political power by default. As stated in Wikipedia Encyclopedia:

> Gregory's action in appointing governors to cities, providing munitions" of war, giving instructions to generals, sending ambassadors to the Lombard king, and even negotiating a peace without consulting the Emperor's legate, Romanus, Exarch of Ravenna, mark the decisive acts
>
> [24] "that revealed the papacy as an independent temporal power]

His development of the doctrine of purgatory was instrumental in establishing the medieval Roman Catholic sacramental system.

From Gregory until the Reformation, true believers were persecuted, and many were martyred for their faith. The Roman Catholic Church was not only recognized by the Roman Empire at that time, but the State was ultimately compelled to bow to the edicts of the Church.

From here we can date practically all the false doctrines of the Roman Church which will be discussed in detail later.

Examination of Their Beliefs

MANY OF THE OFFICIAL doctrines of the Roman Catholic Church are either unbiblical or extra-biblical.

The Catholics use a different Bible than the Protestants and Baptists. Their Bible includes the Apocrypha, which accounts for some of the differences in Catholic doctrines.

Furthermore, the Catholic Church has traditionally held that salvation can be attained only through observance of its sacraments. Therefore, it has set itself apart as the only true church and only true salvation.

Within Catholicism, the definitions related to salvation are different, and salvation is based on works. Because of this, Catholics do not believe that anyone can be assured of their salvation.

Redefining Biblical Terms
Grace

- *Bible*: God's disposition toward mankind, wherein He expresses His mercy and love so that the believer is now treated *as if* he were innocent and righteous.

- *Catholicism*: A power - separate from God - which is placed into a believer. This power enables the believer to perform works that will earn him or her the "right" to heaven.

Salvation

- *Bible*: The instantaneous reception of an irrevocable right standing before God. Salvation is secured by faith, through the grace of God. Romans 3:23 tells us that "*all have sinned and fall short of the glory of God.*" Salvation is given to those the Bible describes as "ungodly," "sinners," "enemies," and "children of wrath."

- *Catholicism*: The lifelong process whereby God and men cooperate in the securing of forgiveness of sin. This is achieved only after death (and/or cleansing from sin in purgatory), and is dependent on man's securing of objective righteousness before God; otherwise, there would be no salvation.

Reconciliation (atonement for sins)

- *Bible:* All sins are forgiven at the point of salvation because Christ's death satisfied all God's wrath against sin. (Col 2:13,14)

- *Catholicism:* Sins are only potentially forgiven, and so must be worked off through a process mediated by the Church and its sacraments over the lifetime of the believer.

Regeneration

- *Bible:* The instantaneous imparting of eternal life and the quickening of the human spirit, making it alive to God by his Spirit.

- *Catholicism:* The lifelong process of infusing grace (spiritual power) to perform meritorious works (in part).

Justification

- *Bible:* The legal declaration of Christ's righteousness reckoned to the believer at the point of faith, solely as an act of God's mercy.

- *Catholicism:* Spiritual rebirth and the lifelong process of sanctification which begins at the point of the sacrament of baptism.

Seven Sacraments

The Catholics maintain that these sacraments are necessary for salvation, but not all are necessary for each person. For example, Holy orders would only be necessary for those in Church leadership.

- ***Baptism*** - cleanses from original sin, removes other sin and its punishment, provides spiritual rebirth or regeneration, begins the process of justification, and is necessary for salvation.

- ***Confirmation*** - bestows the Holy Spirit on Catholics, leading to an increase of sanctifying grace, the gifts of the Holy Spirit, other spiritual powers, and a sealing to the Catholic Church.

- ***Penance*** - removes the penalty of sins committed after baptism and confirmation. Thus, mortal (deadly) sins are remitted, and the justification lost by such sins is restored as a continuing process.

- ***Holy Eucharist*** - where Christ is sacrificed again and the benefits of Calvary are continually applied anew to the believer.

- *Marriage* - where grace is given to remain in the bonds of matrimony in dictates with the requirements of the Catholic Church.

- *Anointing the sick* (formerly extreme unction) - bestows grace on those who are sick, old, or near death and helps in the forgiveness of sins and sometimes the physical healing of the body.

- *Holy orders* - confer special grace and spiritual power upon bishops, priests, and deacons for leadership in the Church as representatives of Christ for all eternity.

Mariolotry

Catholics say that they do not worship Mary; however, a simple visit to the Catholic Encyclopedia makes it very clear. She is listed as "Mary, the Mother of Jesus Christ, the Mother of God".[25]

Note this quote from another article: "In the Constitution Ineffabilis Deus of 8 December 1854, Pius IX pronounced and defined that the Blessed Virgin Mary "in the first instance of her conception, by a singular privilege and grace granted by God, in view of the merits of Jesus Christ, the Saviour of the human race, was preserved exempt from all stain of original sin."

They even have a special prayer that clearly states that Mary can intercede for sin:

> *HAIL MARY, full of grace, the Lord is with thee. Blessed art thou among women, and blessed is the fruit of thy womb, Jesus. Holy Mary, Mother of God, pray for us sinners [emphasis mine], now and at the hour of our death. Amen.*

Purgatory

According to Catholic doctrine, the blood of Jesus cleanses us from original sin – that is, the sin inherent in humans that occurred via the fall in the Garden of Eden.

Each individual commits sins on top of the original sin, for which only the sinner may atone. This is achieved partly through penance and adherence to the sacraments during their lifetime.

The remaining blemishes of sin must be cleansed through the fires of purgatory, before entering heaven.

The "proofs" used by the Catholic Church to support the doctrine of purgatory come from Catholic Tradition and the Apocrypha.

Scripture

Catholics believe in the Bible (or at least their version of it, with several extra books added) but contend that Catholic Tradition (decrees of the various popes and councils) is equal to the Bible.

The Catholic Encyclopedia describes the Christian view of biblical infallibility as follows: "The belief in the Bible as the sole source of faith is unhistorical, illogical, fatal to the virtue of faith, and destructive of unity."

Clearly, then, Catholicism places tradition above Scripture.

Catholics occasionally will speak of the "perspicuity" of Scripture, but in a different way than we would use the term because Scripture only becomes truly clear when understood in the interpretive framework provided by the Church.

The Church

Catholics believe in a universal church body under the head of the Pope.

One becomes a member of this "body" by observance of the sacraments.

Salvation

The Catholic Church says they believe a person must be born again to be saved. However, Catholics believe that one is born again at Baptism.

Biblical Analysis

THE ISSUE CONCERNING any church and its practices should be, "Is this biblical?" If the teaching is biblical (taken in context), it should be embraced. If it is not, it should be rejected.

Jesus was very concerned about abandoning the Word of God to follow the traditions of men.

> *Mark 7:7 Howbeit in vain do they worship me, teaching for doctrines the commandments of men.*

Traditions are not inherently wrong. Some are good and valuable. Some are not. Again, the issue must be whether a doctrine, practice, or tradition is Biblical.

How then does the Roman Catholic Church compare with the teachings of the Word of God?

Salvation (Heresy)

The Roman Catholic Church teaches that salvation is by baptismal regeneration and is maintained through the Catholic sacraments unless a willful act of sin is committed that breaks the state of sanctifying grace.

The Bible teaches that we are saved by grace, which is received through simple faith (Ephesians 2:8-9), and that good works are the result of a change of the heart wrought in salvation (Ephesians 2:10; 2 Corinthians 5:17) and the fruit of that new life in Christ (John 15).

Assurance of Salvation (Error)

The Roman Catholic Church teaches that salvation cannot be guaranteed or assured.

1 John 5:13 states that the letter of 1 John was written to assure believers of the *certainty* of their salvation.

Good Works (Heresy)

The Roman Catholic Church states that Christians are saved by meritorious works (beginning with baptism) and that salvation is maintained by good works (receiving the sacraments, confession of sin to a priest, etc.)

The Bible states that Christians are saved by grace through faith, totally apart from works (Titus 3:5; Ephesians 2:8-9; Galatians 3:10-11; Romans 3:19-24).

Baptism (Heresy)

In the New Testament baptism is **always** practiced **after** saving faith in Christ. Baptism is not the means of salvation; it is faith in the Gospel that saves (1 Corinthians 1:14-18; Romans 10:13-17).

The Roman Catholic Church teaches baptismal regeneration of infants, a practice never found in Scripture. Their support comes from Acts 16:33 which does not even mention infants. Additionally, the context of Acts 16:31 points to salvation through faith!

Prayer (Error)

The Roman Catholic Church teaches Catholics to not only pray to God but also to petition Mary and the saints for their prayers.

Contrary to this, we are taught in Scripture to only pray to God (Matthew 6:9; Luke 18:1-7).

Priesthood (Error)

The Roman Catholic Church teaches that there is a distinction between the clergy and the "lay people," whereas the New Testament teaches the priesthood of all believers (1 Peter 2:9).

Sacraments (Heresy)

The Roman Catholic Church teaches that a believer is infused with grace upon reception of the sacraments.

Such teaching is nowhere found in Scripture. Rather grace is a free gift of God (John 1:17; Romans 12:3, 6; 15:15; 1 Corinthians 1:4; 3:10; Galatians 2:9; Ephesians 3:2, 7, 8; 4:7; 2 Timothy 1:9)

Confession (Heresy)

The Roman Catholic Church teaches that unless a believer is hindered, the only way to receive the forgiveness of sins is by confessing them to a priest.

Contrary to this, Scripture teaches that confession of sins is to be made to God (1 John 1:9).

Mary (Heresy)

The Roman Catholic Church teaches, among other things, that Mary is the Queen of Heaven, a perpetual virgin, and the co-redemptress who ascended into heaven.

In Scripture, she is portrayed as an obedient, believing servant of God, who became the mother of Jesus. None of the other attributes mentioned by the Roman Catholic Church have any basis in the Bible.

The idea of Mary being the co-redemptress and another mediator between God and man is not only extra-biblical (found only outside of Scripture) but is also unbiblical (Acts 4:12; 1 Timothy 2:5)

Many other examples could be given. These issues alone clearly identify the Catholic Church as being a cult.

Every Christian denomination has traditions and practices that are not explicitly based on Scripture. That is why Scripture must be the standard of Christian faith and practice.

The Word of God is always true and reliable. The same cannot be said of church tradition. Our guideline is to be: "What does Scripture say?" (Romans 4:3; Galatians 4:30; Acts 17:11).

Mormonism - Church of Jesus Christ of Latter-Day Saints

The Mormon religion is founded upon their so-called Prophet, Joseph Smith.

Joseph Smith was born on December 23, 1805, in Sharon, Vermont. In 1820, when he was only 14-15 years old, he claimed to have a vision telling him that all churches were in error and that he should join none of them.

In 1823, he had a second vision in which a messenger named Moroni appeared to him, telling him the location of a book written on golden plates.

Smith supposedly found the plates at a site known as the hill Cumorah, but he was not allowed to remove them at that time. Finally, he says, the heavenly messenger gave him the plates on September 21st, 1823.

Smith began translating the plates, and on March 26, 1830, with the financial help of a farmer named Martin Harris, he published the Book of Mormon. Joseph Smith provided nine different versions of these events, which set the tone for the rest of his teachings.

The Latter-day Saints Church was organized in April 1830. Some of Smith's followers went to Kirtland, Ohio, where a Temple was built. Later, Mormons moved onward to Independence, Missouri.

Smith received a revelation that Jackson County (Independence, Missouri) was the land of promise and the place for the city of Zion. However, he and his followers were not well received, and they moved to Far West, Missouri, and then to a community in Illinois which they called Nauvoo.

Smith found himself in trouble after the Nauvoo Expositor, an anti-Mormon paper, published negative information about him. He then ordered his men to destroy and burn every issue they could find.

When the owners of the paper took this information to the Governor, Smith was arrested.

He was later released and then shortly thereafter was re-arrested along with his brother Hyrum, and was taken to the county jail in Carthage, Illinois.

On June 27, 1844, a mob attacked the jail and killed both Joseph and Hyrum Smith. This act inadvertently turned Smith into a martyred hero in the eyes of his followers, serving as a disservice to the opponents of Mormonism. [26]

After this, the Mormons split into two groups. The group that followed Brigham Young went on to Salt Lake City, Utah.

The smaller group, known as the Reorganized Church of Jesus Christ of Latter-Day Saints, went back to Independence, Missouri.

Doctrinal Beliefs

A PARTIAL LIST OF SOME of the more well-known doctrinal problems and Scriptures that refute it:

- There are many gods,[27] and a faithful Mormon man can eventually become a god. Ephesians 4:6, Matthew 28:19, and Exodus 20:1-7.

- The Bible was only the first revelation, so we also need the Book of Mormon. Revelation 22:18-19, and John 12:48.

- Salvation is the resurrection of the dead. John 5:28-29, and Revelation 20:11-15.

- One can be baptized for the dead to save them. Romans 10:14-17, Romans 14:12, Mark 16:15-16, and Acts 2:38.

- Water[28] is to be used as the blood in the Lord's Supper. Matthew 26:29, and Mark 14:22-25.

- Marriage is eternal. Romans 7:2-3, Matthew 22:23-33.

- The Church would fall and there would be a need for restoring it to a new faith. Hebrews 12:28, Matthew 28:20.

- Joseph Smith said that all Christian denominations were "wrong ... all their creeds were an abomination in his sight, and that those professors (Christians) were all corrupt" (*Pearl of Great Price, Joseph Smith, 2:18-19*).

• Prophets exist today. II Peter 1:3.

The Book of Mormon Versus The Bible

THE CLAIM IS OFTEN made by the Mormons that the Bible and the Book of Mormon are completely compatible, that is, that there are no contradictions. But note the following:

• *Priests of Aaron or Joseph?*

The Bible affirms that only those of Aaron's descent were to be priests (Numbers 3:10).

The Book of Mormon states in 2 Nephi 5:26, "I, Nephi, did consecrate Jacob and Joseph, that they should be priests . . .." These supposed men were descendants of Levi (1 Nephi 18:7) who was of the tribe of Joseph (1 Nephi 6:14). It seems that Mormonism also "walks in the ways of Jeroboam" (1 Kings 12:31).

• *Is the Bible Complete or Not?*

The Bible claims to be the complete (Jude 3) and all-sufficient (2 Timothy 3:16,17; 2 Peter 1:3) Word of God.

The Book of Mormon ridicules one who would make such a claim (2 Nephi 29:3) and denies that it contains all of God's written revelation to man (2 Nephi 29:6,10).

• *Gospel Spread from Jerusalem or Not?*

The Bible in Luke 24:46-47 states very clearly that "repentance and remission of sins should be preached in his name among all nations, beginning at Jerusalem." Such was fulfilled in Acts 2.

The Book of Mormon has this occurring in 2 Nephi 31:11-17 which claims to be between 559 and 545 B.C. and thousands of miles away from Jerusalem!

• *"Will Build" or "Already There"?*

The Bible records that the Lord plainly affirmed while upon this earth that he would build his church (Matthew 16:18).

The Book of Mormon states, "They were called the church of God, or the church of Christ, from that time forward." (Mosiah 18:17). This supposedly occurred about 147 B.C.!

• *Jerusalem or Bethlehem?*

The Bible tells us that Jesus was born in Bethlehem (Micah 5:2; Matthew 2:1).

The Book of Mormon says "he shall be born of Mary at Jerusalem" (Alma 7:10). Lest they say that Jerusalem is an area and not a city, in 1 Nephi 1:4 their own writing calls it a city.

• *First in Antioch or the Americas?*

The Bible affirms that the "disciples were called Christians first in Antioch" (Acts 11:26).

The Book of Mormon misses that by several thousand miles and nearly 100 years in having believers in Christ called Christians in 73 B.C. (Alma 46:15).

• *Zedekiah's Son Lived in America?*

The Bible tells us in 2 Kings 25:7 "They slew the sons of Zedekiah before his eyes."

The Book of Mormon has one supposed son of Zedekiah (Mulek) living in the Americas (Heleman 8:21).

• *3 Days or 3 Hours?*

The Bible records in Mark 15:33 that at Jesus' crucifixion, there was darkness for 3 hours.

The Book of Mormon has darkness for 3 days (3 Nephi 8:20-23).

• *"Until" or Go For Visits?*

The Bible tells us in Acts 2:34-35 and 3:20-21 that Jesus is to remain in heaven after his ascension "until" his foes are made his footstool, and "until the times of restitution."

The Book of Mormon has him appearing in the Americas after his ascension (3 Nephi 10:18-19).

More could be said about how the Book of Mormon does not agree with the Bible, but this is sufficient to show that one cannot take both as being the Word of God.

The Book of Mormon Versus Itself

ONE OF THE SEVERAL proofs of the Bible is its unity; there are no contradictions within it. Such cannot be said of the Book of Mormon.

• *Is The Book of Mormon Divine or Not?*

On the title page of the Book of Mormon we find the claim that it was "Written by way of commandment and also by the spirit of prophecy and of revelation," and even "the interpretation thereof by the gift of God." Unbelievably in the very next paragraph, we find the statement, "And now if there are faults they are the mistakes of men!" It even gets worse after that.

Again in the same book in chapter 19, we find Nephi being told to make a record. Of his ability to do this he says, "Nevertheless, I do not write anything upon plates save it be that I think it be sacred. And now, if I do err, even did they err of old . . ." (1 Nephi 19:6)

• *Is baptism essential for Salvation or not?*

In 3 Nephi 11:33,3, we find the teaching that baptism is essential to one's salvation,"..whoso believeth not in me, and is not baptized, shall be damned."

Just a few chapters earlier we read of those that "should be baptized with water, and this as a witness and a testimony before God, and unto the people, that they had repented and received remission of their sins" (3 Nephi 7:25)

• *Flesh and blood or Spirit?*

Alma 22:9-11 teaches that God is a Spirit.

Ether 3:9 (and also Doctrine and Covenants 130:22) teaches that He is flesh and blood! [29]

Biblical Analysis

DEUTERONOMY 18:22 GIVES God's standards for His prophets: 100% accuracy. Joseph Smith wrote a lot of prophecies, many of which never came true. He was a false prophet, and the religion he founded was not from God.

Mormonism denies the deity of Christ. The Bible clearly teaches it (John 1:1,14; John 10:30; Heb 1:3,8).

To the Mormons, Jesus is the firstborn son of an exalted "man" who became the god of this world. The man-god of Mormonism was made the god of this world because of his good works on another planet somewhere out in the universe.

He "earned" godhood, and was thus appointed by a council of gods in the heavens to his high position as the god of planet Earth. The Mormon god of this world was a man, like all men, who became a god.

Mormons believe that man may attain godhood. The Scriptures teach quite the opposite (Gen 3:5; Eze 28:9; Num 23:19; Isa 44:6; Rom 1:22)!

This is what the celestial marriage and the temple vows are all about. LDS men, by doing their temple work, are striving for exaltation by which they, too, shall one day become gods.

Their wives will be the mother goddesses of "their" world and with their husbands, will produce the population of their world. This is the Mormon doctrine of "eternal progression."

Note the following quote from the Mormon Journal of Discourses, vol. 1, page 123, made by the LDS Apostle Orson Hyde: "Remember that God, our heavenly Father, was perhaps once a child, a mortal like we ourselves, and rose step by step in the scale of progress, in the school of advancement; has moved forward and overcome, until He has arrived at the point where He is."

The Jesus Christ of Mormonism is not the Jesus Christ of the Bible. The Mormon Jesus is the son of this man-god. The Mormon Jesus is the brother of Lucifer, and according to LDS teaching, he married several of the Marys of the New Testament. He is not, to the LDS church, "God incarnate" as the Bible plainly states.

Orson Hyde, the Mormon Apostle said, "We say it was Jesus Christ who was married in the marriage of Cana of Galilee" (Journal of Discourses, Vol. 2, page 80).

Brigham Young, said, "When the Virgin Mary conceived the Child Jesus ... He was not begotten by the Holy Ghost. And who is His father? He is the first of the human family" (Journal of Discourses, pages 50-51).

Note Luke 1:35.

Luke 1:35 And the angel answered and said unto her, The Holy Ghost shall come upon thee, and the power of the Highest shall overshadow thee: therefore also that holy thing which shall be born of thee shall be called the Son of God.

Either the Bible is true or it is not. But both cannot be true!

Mormons teach that to place faith in the atonement of Christ's blood will cause one to lose his salvation.

Note the following quote from, "What Mormons Think of Christ" (LDS publication, pages 32-34): "Christians speak often of the blood of Christ and its cleansing power. Much is believed and taught on this subject, however, it is utter nonsense and so palpably false that to believe it is to lose one's salvation."

The Bible teaches atonement only through the blood of Christ. (1 John 1:7; Heb 9:14; Rev 1:5)

Mormons believe in a "works-based" salvation. (Eph 2:8-9; Rom 4:5).

Belief in the real Jesus Christ is the only way a man can receive forgiveness of sin and eternal life. The LDS, in presenting a false Christ is leading souls away from salvation and the real Jesus. They reject God's truth and substitute another Jesus who does not exist and cannot save.

The history of Jehovah's Witnesses dates back to 1872, when Charles Taze Russell began leading a Bible study group in Pittsburgh, Pennsylvania.

In 1870, he met Advent Christian preacher Jonas Wendell (one of the Millerites' spiritual heirs) and organized a Bible study group in Pittsburgh, Pennsylvania.

Russell obtained many of his ideas from Adventists and others who speculated on Bible prophecy.

In 1884, Russell founded the Watchtower Society, which became the legal corporation used by the International Bible Students, the early name for Jehovah's Witnesses. His Watchtower Bible and Tract Society have produced a prodigious amount of literature.

In 1876, Russell met Nelson H. Barbour and adopted Barbour's understanding of biblical chronology, originally published by Christopher Bowen in 1861. Barbour (like Wendell) had predicted a visible return of Christ for 1873, and when that failed, revised the prediction to 1874.

Russell broke with Barbour in July 1879 over the concept of substitutionary atonement. He soon began publishing his own magazine, Zion's Watch Tower and Herald of Christ's Presence (now known as The Watchtower).

He retained Barbour's teaching that the "end times" had begun in 1799 and that Christ had returned invisibly in 1874. 1878 became the date for Christ's enthronement as king, the resurrection of the saints, and God's judgment of Christendom. 1914 was held as the ending date of a harvest period that would culminate in Armageddon.

Originally known as the Bible Students (this was literally the name they wanted for themselves!), they experienced a major schism in 1917 as Joseph Franklin Rutherford began his presidency after Russell's death in 1916.

Rutherford stressed 1925 as a date for Armageddon. When nothing supernatural happened in 1925, the Watchtower Society lost three-quarters of its members.

Rutherford gave the movement a new direction and coined the name "Jehovah's Witnesses" in 1931. Following his death, Nathan Knorr took over the presidency of the Watchtower Bible and Tract Society.

Later, 1975 was heavily stressed as a possible date for Armageddon. In 1976, leadership of the Jehovah's Witness movement began to be directed by a Governing Body.

The Watchtower Bible and Tract Society claim it is the sole information channel between God and humanity.

Charles Taze Russell had been held to be the "Faithful and Wise Servant" of Matthew 24:45-47, but by 1928, the Society applied that to numerous leaders. They taught that the scripture was a prophecy and that in 1918 they had been chosen by Jesus "over all that he hath."

Since they believed Jesus was ruling the world invisibly, they claimed for themselves the prestige of being the sole channel of information from God to man.

Doctrinal Differences

THE DIFFERENCES IN doctrine are many and varied, and the following table lists only a few of the major differences:

The Bible	Jehovah's Witnesses teaching
Nature of God	
God has revealed Himself as the Father, the Son and the Holy Spirit. They are one God. Jesus (the Son) is God in the flesh. During his life on earth he was both fully God and fully human. He is eternal and equal in power to God.	Only the Father (Jehovah) is God.
	Jesus is God's Son, but not God. He was created by Jehovah as the archangel Michael before the physical world existed, and is a lesser god.
The Holy Spirit is a person of the Trinity. The Holy Spirit is eternal and equal in power to God.	The holy spirit is God's impersonal, "active force".
Jesus	
Jesus is God's Son. He is God in the flesh.	Jesus is God's Son, and is a god (or divine being); but not God Himself. Jesus is also the archangel Michael in his pre-human existence, as well as Apollyon/Abaddon, mentioned in Revelation 9:11.
Jesus was crucified on a cross.	Jesus was nailed to a torture stake.
Jesus' body was resurrected (Luke 24:39; cf. John 2:19-21).	Jesus' body was not resurrected; he was resurrected as a spirit.
The return of Christ to the earth will be physical, and has not yet occurred.	The return of Christ occurred invisibly in 1914.
Death/Afterlife	
The human soul is eternal and does not	The soul ceases to exist when a person dies, requiring a resurrection to live again.

cease to exist at any time.

| Immediately following death, there is afterlife for all mankind in heaven or Hell. | There is no spiritual afterlife immediately following death, except for the 144,000, who are immediately taken to heaven. Hell is mankind's common grave. |
| The unrighteous will be tormented in hell for eternity. | There is no eternal torment. Those who have committed an unforgivable sin experience 'Gehenna' (eternal destruction or extinction) at death. |

Judgment and Salvation

| All who are saved (born again) will spend eternity in heaven with God. | Only 144,000 are born again and will spend eternity in heaven ruling over the Earth with Jesus Christ. With the exception of those who have experienced Gehenna, all who have died (both righteous and unrighteous) will be resurrected with the potential to live forever on a paradise earth. |
| To be saved, a person must believe in Jesus Christ. | To be considered righteous, a person must obey Jesus' commands, dedicate himself to Jehovah, and serve God as part of Jehovah's Witnesses. |

A.

Unfulfilled Predictions

Predictions such as the following have appeared in various Watchtower publications:

1907: Armageddon will culminate in the year 1914.

1917: In 1918, God would begin to destroy churches "wholesale" and church members by the millions.

1922-1923: The resurrection of the dead would occur in 1925. In preparation for this date, the Watchtower Society acquired a property in California and built a mansion on it. The mansion was to house people such as Abraham, Moses, David, and Samuel, whom they thought would be resurrected to life in 1925. Interestingly,

Jospeh Franklin Rutherford used the mansion during the winter months for "health reasons."

1938: In 1938, Armageddon was too close for marriage or childbearing.

1941: There were only "months" remaining until Armageddon.

1942: Armageddon was "immediately before us."

1969: Human existence would not last long enough for young people to grow old; the world system would end "in a few years." For this reason, Young Witnesses were encouraged not to bother pursuing tertiary education.

1969: Christ's thousand-year reign would begin in 1975. In the decade or so leading up to 1975, Watchtower publications speculated extensively about this.

1984: There were "many indications" that "the end" was closer than the end of the 20th century.

Biblical Analysis

DENIAL OF THE AUTHORITY of Scripture

Under the leadership of Nathan H. Knorr (1905-1977), the Watchtower Society temporarily abandoned date setting and switched to a different strategy.

Since many of their teachings are easily refuted by key verses in the King James Bible, Knorr set out to publish a different Bible for Jehovah's Witnesses to use.

The Watchtower Society Bible, called the New World Translation (NWT), blatantly alters many verses that show the errors of Watchtower's teaching.

The single best example of this is John 1:1, which, in the King James Version, declares Jesus' deity—"the Word was God." The Watchtower Society denies Christ's deity, so the NWT renders this phrase "the Word was a god."

Another example is found in the Old Testament book of Zechariah 12:10. Jehovah God is speaking and says, "*They shall look upon **me** whom they have pierced*," understood by Christians as a predictive reference to the crucifixion. Recognizing that Jesus' fulfillment of this prophecy would mean that he is Jehovah God, the Watchtower Society has changed this verse in the NWT to read "They will certainly look to the One whom they pierced through," thus eliminating another reference to the deity of Jesus Christ.

The Society made similar changes to many other verses relating to the deity of Christ (Colossians 1:16-20; Titus 2:13; Hebrews 1:8).

They have also altered verses that expose the Watchtower Society's false teaching on subjects like the reality of eternal punishment (Matthew 25:46).

More changes were made concerning the personality of the Holy Spirit (1 Corinthians 14:14-16; 1 Timothy 4:1; Jude 19).

In this way, the Watchtower Society gives Jehovah's Witnesses and potential converts the illusion that the Bible supports its erroneous doctrines.

The Bible teaches that the Holy Spirit's anointing enables individual Christians to understand God's Word and properly apply it to their lives (John 16:13; 1 John 2:27). By contrast, the Watchtower Society teaches that the Bible can only be interpreted by the Watchtower Society, and no individual can learn the truth apart from them.

The Nature of God.

The Watchtower Society denies God's triune nature and teaches that such a belief is inspired by Satan. It teaches that Jehovah, the name of the one true God, corresponds only to God the Father. The Society also denies that Jesus is God. They deny the Holy Spirit is a person and instead teach that he is merely God's active force, analogous to electricity.

The Bible teaches that there is only one true God (Isaiah 43:10-11; 44:6,8). Father, Son, and Holy Spirit are identified as distinct Persons within the one Triune Godhead (Matthew 3:16-17; 2 Corinthians 13:14). Throughout the New Testament, the Son and the Holy Spirit, as well as the Father, are separately identified as God. The attributes and prerogatives of Deity are ascribed to each (Son: Mark 2:5-12; John 20:28; Hebrews 1:8; Holy Spirit: Acts 5:3-4; 2 Corinthians 3:17-18).

The Doctrine of Christ

The Watchtower Society denies the deity of Jesus Christ and teaches that Jesus is a created being. He first existed as Michael the Archangel and later was born as a perfect man. Jehovah's Witnesses believe that after Jesus was buried, God disposed of his physical body. Jesus was raised as a spirit creature and "materialized" a fleshly body to make himself visible. Now, in heaven, he is again known as Michael the Archangel.

The Bible teaches that Jesus Christ is God come in the flesh and is the Creator of all things (John 1:1-3, 14; Col. 1:16). While never less than God, at the appointed time, He laid aside the glory He shared with the Father and took on human nature (John 17:3-5; Phil. 2:6-11; Col. 2:9). Following his death, Jesus Christ rose bodily from the grave, appeared to and was recognized in his body by over 500 people. (Luke 24:39; John 2:19-21; 1 Corinthians 15:6, 14).

The Doctrine of Salvation

The Watchtower Society teaches that only an elite group of Witnesses, known as "the 144,000," or the "anointed ones," are presently credited with Christ's righteousness. Only the 144,000 are born again and expect to reign with Christ in heaven. For the vast majority of the remaining Jehovah's Witnesses, known as the "other sheep" or the "great crowd," the atoning sacrifice of Christ only provides a chance at eternal life on earth.

The Bible teaches that the atoning work of Christ alone provides the solution for man's sin problem. Jesus Christ took the personal sins of all men — past, present, and future — in his own body on the tree (1 Peter 2:24), and as perfect God and perfect man, he fully met the demands of Divine justice for us (Romans 3:22-26). Therefore, all who receive him by simple faith (John 1:12; Acts 16:31) can be forgiven, declared righteous, and restored to fellowship with God (2 Corinthians 5:21; Hebrews 7:24-26).

The Bible also teaches that we are saved by grace alone, apart from any self-righteous works; salvation is God's gift. There is nothing we can do to contribute to our salvation because apart from Jesus Christ, we are "dead in our sins" (Ephesians 2:1-9).

By contrast, the Watchtower Society teaches that we must earn our own salvation; salvation will "depend on one's works." A person must first "come to Jehovah's organization for salvation" and then comply with everything they teach. In this way, a relationship with the Jehovah's Witnesses organization, rather than a personal relationship with Jesus Christ, is presented as the basis of salvation.

The Soul, Spirit, and Eternal Punishment

The Watchtower Society denies eternal punishment and teaches that man does not have a spirit that survives the death of the body. Witnesses believe that death ends all conscious existence. Hell refers to the grave, and those who are ultimately judged by God will be annihilated and simply cease to exist.

The Bible teaches that the human spirit continues to exist consciously after death (Luke 16:19-31; 2 Corinthians 5:6, 8; Philippians 1:23-24; Rev. 6:9-11). Those who have rejected God's gift of eternal life will suffer conscious eternal punishment (Matthew 25:41,46; Revelation 14:10,11; 20:10,15).

The Unification Church (UC) believes that Jesus appeared to Mun Yong-myong (his birth name) on April 17, 1935, when Moon was 15 years old.

They believe Jesus asked him to accomplish the work left unaccomplished after his crucifixion. This should set off warning bells for any thinking believer. The implication is that Jesus' work was insufficient.

After a period of prayer and consideration, Moon accepted the mission, later changing his name to Mun Son-myong (Sun Myung Moon).

Moon's studies took him to the southern part of Korea (North and South Korea were one country then) and Japan, where he studied electrical engineering. During this same time, Moon reports to have received visions from various religious leaders including Jesus and Buddha.

After finishing his studies, he moved back to Korea. He was arrested and tortured at the hands of North Korean authorities primarily due to his religious activities and his perceived opposition to the North Korean regime. The regime viewed religious leaders and organizations as threats to its control and ideology.

Then, he moved to Pyongyang, where he established the Broad Sea Church.

Between 1946 and 1950, he gathered a following and was imprisoned multiple times for political and religious reasons.

The official beginning was on May 1, 1954. The church's teachings are based on Moon's interpretation of the Bible, which he outlined in the book "Divine Principle." The church aimed to promote world peace and unity through spiritual and moral renewal.

The Divine Principle first saw written form as Wolli Wonbon in 1946. The second, expanded version, Wolli Hesol, or Explanation of the Divine Principle, was published in 1957.

Sun Myung Moon preached in northern Korea after the end of World War II and was imprisoned by the communist regime in North Korea in 1946. He was released from prison, along with many North Koreans, with the advance of American and United Nations forces during the Korean War.

As a refugee in Pusan, he built his first church from mud and cardboard boxes.

Moon formally founded his organization in Seoul, Korea, on May 1, 1954, calling it "The Holy Spirit Association for the Unification of World Christianity." The name alludes to Moon's stated intention for his organization to be a unifying force for all Christian denominations.

"Unification" has political and religious connotations, in keeping with the church's teaching that restoration must be complete—both spiritual and physical.

In 1958, Moon sent missionaries to Japan, and in 1959, to America. Moon himself moved to the United States in 1971.

UC missionaries found success in San Francisco first, where it expanded in both Berkeley and San Francisco as the Creative Community Project.

By 1973, UC missions had spread to most of the nation's populous cities.

In 1975, Moon sent out missionaries to 120 countries to spread the Unification Church around the world and also in part, he said, to act as "lightning rods" to receive "persecution."

Since this time, the "Moonies" have grown immensely, both financially as well as numerically, largely through their aggressive proselytizing programs.

Beliefs

SOURCE OF AUTHORITY.

The Moonies teach that the Bible is "not the truth itself, but a textbook teaching the truth."

Moon's 536-page spiritual manifesto, Divine Principle (1957), is considered to be their scriptures (supposedly revealed directly to Moon by Jesus Christ), along with the Bible.

Divine Principle is considered to be the "third testament" of the Bible and superior to it. The Unification Church also believes in continuing revelation.

Moon claims to have received new revelations from God, i.e., "I spoke with Jesus Christ in the spirit world. And I also spoke with John the Baptist. This is my authority."

Even the Divine Principle is not the complete truth. "The Divine Principle revealed in this book is only part of the new truth. ... as time goes on, deeper parts of the truth will be continually revealed" (Unification Theology, p. 16).

Ultimately, Moon's interpretations and teachings are considered the final and absolute source of authority. Any person harboring doubts about Moon is deemed to be allowing himself to be part of the work of Satan.

Method of Interpretation.

The Moonies interpret much of the Bible allegorically; they teach that the thieves on the cross represent democracy (the "right") and Communism (the "left").

They claim that "resurrection" does not refer to raising the dead but to accepting the "word of God" (1 Corinthians 15:12-20).

Moon also believes the Bible teaches that Christianity is not the only divinely revealed and saving faith.

Dualism and the fall.

Moonies believe that everything in existence has a dual aspect, including God.

They claim that God originally intended for Adam and Eve to have a brother/sister relationship until they reached perfection and that Adam and Eve were supposed to establish God's kingdom on earth through marriage and childbearing.

Therefore, the Fall was the result of sexual sin; i.e., that Eve had sexual relations with Satan (the spiritual fall) and then with Adam (the physical fall).

The Occult.

Moon admits communicating with familiar spirits through séances.

Though the Christian ordinances of baptism and communion are avoided by the Unification Church, it readily accepts clairvoyance, automatic handwriting, and mediumistic trances.

Sin.

Unification theology teaches that Adam and Eve's fall came not from disobedience in eating fruit from the tree of knowledge but was sexual in nature.

According to Moon, then, sin is a matter of genetics (physical children of Lucifer), not a moral choice.

Salvation, therefore, requires physical redemption; i.e. it is a matter of being born of Moon's physical bond or entering a marriage union chosen and blessed by Moon himself.

And then there is the completely wacky teaching of "blood cleansing". Originally, "Blood cleansing," as defined by Moon, was accomplished for any male by having sexual relations with a woman that had been "cleansed" by Moon.

So, to put this into plain terms, Moon would sleep with a woman first, and then she could, in turn, sleep with another man.

Now, those who submit to Moon's authority (e.g., by turning over all financial assets to the Unification Church, allowing Moon to choose one's mate, etc.) may consider their devotion a spiritual kind of purification not requiring sexual cohabitation.

God the Father.

"Unification theology asserts that God has masculine and feminine qualities based on the universal fact of polarity ..."

There are similarities between the Unification Church theology of God the Father and the deity concept of I Ching, Confucianism, Taoism, and Hinduism.

"God must exist in polarity. He must possess within Himself the dual characteristics of masculinity and femininity, perfectly expressed and fully harmonized in His nature. The doctrine of divine polarity taught by Unification theology should be seen not as an eccentric novelty but as a reaffirmation of a valid theological insight" (Unification Theology, p. 56).

Jesus Christ.

Moonies deny the deity of Jesus Christ; instead, they claim He was just a man, not God. ("God is just like you and me. All human traits originate in God."—Moon, Christianity in Crisis, p. 4; and "He can by no means be God Himself."—Divine Principle, pp. 210-211).

They teach that Jesus was not virgin-born but was the illegitimate offspring of Zechariah and Mary! They also claim that Jesus failed in His earthly mission (Divine Principle, pp. 143-145) and that Christ's purpose in coming was to marry and produce perfect children.

However, He was killed before He could fulfill His mission (i.e., "The Cross is the symbol of defeat of Christianity," Moon, 1973).

Moonies believe that John the Baptist was responsible for the death of Jesus (by failing to convert his audience into a power bloc for Jesus) (Divine Principle, pp. 156-162), and that Christ's death on the cross was not an original or essential part of God's plan of redemption ("... however devout a man of faith may be, he cannot fulfill physical salvation by redemption through Jesus crucifixion alone."—Divine Principle, p. 148).

They believe that God merely used the cross to provide an incomplete, spiritual salvation.

They do not believe that Jesus was physically resurrected but that He returned as a spirit and that a "third Adam" must come to fulfill God's plan for physical salvation by marrying and producing the sinless race.

The Unification Church has given titles to Moon that indicate it considers him to be this "third Adam."

Salvation

Moonies teach the "Law of Indemnity" - that God's children must pay for at least a part of their debt of sin before God will forgive them.

They believe a person earns salvation through fasting, fund-raising, recruitment, and other such works.

They claim that both spiritual and physical salvation are needed—and that the "third Adam" will provide physical salvation by marrying and producing sinless children (Divine Principle, p. 148).

They teach that once the "third Adam" comes, those who have paid indemnity will also be able to marry and bear sinless children.

Moonies view Moon as that "third Adam" who provides physical salvation through a perfect family (indeed, his twelve children are considered sinless!), and extends this perfection to his followers through their obedience to him.

Holy Spirit.

The Holy Spirit, "... appears feminine, masculine and impersonal. ... Like God Himself, the Spirit is invisible and incorporeal—a bright light or a field of magnetic energy" (Unification Theology, pp. 201-202).

Moonies also teach that the Holy Spirit is a "female spirit"—the "True Mother" and spiritual wife of Jesus (Divine Principle, p. 215).

"She" also cleanses the people's sins to restore them, thus indemnifying the sin committed by Eve.

Trinity

Moonies deny the Biblical concept of the Trinity. They teach that the "third Adam," his bride, and God constituted the first trinity, and that mankind will be restored by forming trinities with God through marriage.

Young Oon Kim, professor of systematic theology at the Unification Theological Seminary, stated, "Unification theology starts with the fact of polarity as the main clue for understanding the essential nature of God. Hence it is not primarily interested in defending the Trinitarian doctrine of the fourth-century creeds" (Unification Theology, p. 53).

Marriage.

Moon teaches that "God-centered families are the building blocks of a world of peace, stability, and love" and that only those who are married will be saved or qualified for the kingdom. (Hence, Moon's fondness for mass marriage ceremonies)

Moon and his wife, Han Hak-ja (wife #4—he divorced the first three), charge each couple an arrangement fee for these mass marriages, which have brought the church more than two billion dollars over the years.

Second Coming.

They deny that Jesus Christ, the Son of God, will return but say that God will send another man as the "third Adam." They deny that the "Christ" will come in the clouds, but instead that he will be born just as Jesus was in the First Advent.

They teach that the Kingdom of God on earth and in heaven will be established by the "third Adam" through marriage.

The bottom line is that they believe that Moon is this "third Adam" and that he has begun to establish God's kingdom—"He [God] is living in me. I am the incarnation of Himself."

Moon says that Jesus failed at the First Coming, but he (Moon) will not! (speech on 8/24/92).

Heaven and Hell.

Moonies teach that heaven is a realm of the spirit world and that hell is inconsequential because it will "pass away as heaven expands," and all mankind is redeemed.

Also, one's destination after death depends on his spirit's "quality of life on earth; by the degree of goodness we build into them through actions."

Rather than immortal perfection, Moon teaches that in the afterlife, his followers will experience the same "desires, dislikes, and aspirations as before death."

Summary

According to Moon, it was God's plan for Jesus to find a perfect mate and produce sinless children, bringing about the world's physical and spiritual salvation. But Jesus failed because He couldn't get the Jews to accept Him as Messiah.

The Crucifixion was a "mistake" that thwarted God's plans and made it necessary for a new Messiah to come during this present age. This new "messiah," called the "Lord of the Second Advent" by Moon, was born in Korea in 1920 (which, coincidentally, is the place and time of his own birth).

Moon claimed that the Messiah would be revealed by the year 2000. (cf. Deut. 18:22). Therefore, Moon does not want us to think of the Second Coming in terms of a literal interpretation of Scripture, which states that Jesus will come in the clouds with great glory.

Moon insists that the second messiah will be a Korean man born of the flesh—and those who do not accept him will face God's wrath.

Accordingly, everyone must be born again by new parents to fulfill God's original plan of redemption. Translated into Moon's theology, this means: that acceptance of Moon and his wife as spiritual parents is necessary for salvation.

Biblical Analysis

SOURCE OF AUTHORITY

The source of all true authority is found in the Bible itself. (Psalm 12:6,7; 19:7,8; 119:9-11, 18, 89, 129, 130, 133, 165; Isaiah 40:8; Mathew 5:18; John 6:68; 8:31,32; 17:17)

In addition, nothing new can be added to the truth that has been delivered to mankind. (Revelation 22:17,18; Deuteronomy 4:2; 12:32; Proverbs 30:6)

Thus, it is a lie to state that any message given by anyone that adds to or contradicts the Scriptures in any way can be from God.

Based upon this alone, Moon Sun Myung must be rejected as a false prophet.

Method of interpretation

Their skills in Scripture interpretation are perhaps the most skewed of all the cults we have studied thus far.

Scripture has much to say about those who wrest the Scriptures to their own destruction. (Jeremiah 23:36; Matthew 15:3-6, Matthew 22:29; 2 Peter 3:16)

Dualism, the Fall and Sin

What sin did Adam and Eve commit? There was only one commandment given to Adam and Eve. They were not to eat of the tree of good and evil.

There was no commandment about not having sex, but precisely the opposite is true.

> **Genesis 1:28** *And God blessed them, and God said unto them, Be fruitful, and multiply, and replenish the earth, and subdue it: and have dominion over the fish of the sea, and over the fowl of the air, and over every living thing that moveth upon the earth.*

In the light of Genesis 2:9, the idea that the tree is a symbol of sex is ludicrous.

"and good for food"... That is what the Bible said about these trees. Not good for pleasure, but for food.

Man is a sinner because he was born with a sinful nature inherited from Adam (Rom 5:12), not because of some mythical union between Eve and Satan.

The Occult

As stated earlier, Scripture is very clear about the involvement of believers with the occult. (see Deuteronomy 18:10-12; Leviticus 19:31; 20:6)

God the Father

There is not one single reference to God as any other quality other than masculine. Every reference is to "He", "Him", and "Father". Isaiah 63:16, 64:8; Act s7:2; 1Corinthians 8:6; Ephesians 4:6; Hebrews 12:9)

The Deity and Sufficiency of Christ

The following list of Scriptures points to the complete sufficiency of Christ. (John 6:35; John 6:53-58; John 8:12; John 10:9-11; John 11:25; John 14:6; John 15:1; John 15:5-7; Colossians 3:4; 2 Timothy 1:10; Revelation 1:18; etc.)

Salvation

As with all the other cults, salvation has always been and always will be by grace through faith. That grace is a gift of God, and the object of that faith is the Lord Jesus Christ himself – certainly not a man!

Trinity

Again, the Scriptures make both plain statements as well as general allusions to the truth of the Trinity. (Gen 1:26; Gen 3:22; Isa 6:3; Isa 6:8; Isa 11:2-3; Isa 42:1; Mat 12:18; Isa 48:16; Isa 61:1-3; Luk 4:18; Isa 63:9-10; Mat 1:18; Mat 1:20; Mat 3:11; Mar 1:8; Luk 3:16; Mat 12:28; Mat 28:19; Luk 1:35; Luk 3:22; Mat 3:16; Luk 4:1; Luk 4:14; Joh 1:32-33; Joh 3:34-35; Joh 7:39; Joh 14:16-17; Joh 14:26; Joh 15:26; Joh 16:7; Joh 16:13-15; Joh 20:22; Act 1:2; Act 1:4-5; Act 2:33; Act 10:36-38; Rom 1:3-4; Rom 8:9-11; Rom 8:26-27; 1Co 2:10-11; 1Co 6:19; 1Co 8:6; 1Co 12:3-6; 2Co 1:21-22; 2Co 5:5; 2Co 3:17; 2Co 13:14; Gal 4:4; Gal 4:6; Phi 1:19; Col 2:2; 2Th 2:13-14; 2Th 2:16; 1Ti 3:16; Tit 3:4-6; Heb 9:14; 1Pe 1:2; 1Pe 3:18; 1Jo 5:6-7; Rev 4:8)

One would have to be in intentional denial to miss this volume of evidence.

What are some of the most dangerous cults?

The Emerging (Emergent) Church Movement

IT IS ALMOST UNBELIEVABLE how subtle and how fast the "emerging church" movement[30] is beginning to affect conservative churches.

The influence is the most obvious among the younger believers. They are becoming increasingly concerned with standards that need a biblical basis. And rightly so.

They are also frustrated with "dinosaur pastors" who fear everything from Facebook to Barnes and Nobles. And I understand both the frustration and the fear.

Bible colleges are not much help. They practically encourage their students to question everything, even the precious doctrines that saints have held on to - even died for - for two thousand years.

In my experience, I have dealt with young men and women from good Bible colleges who have "rethought" issues such as social drinking, gambling, church membership, Calvinism, and even the need for morality in politics!

So, what is wrong with the emerging church?

If New Evangelicalism is dangerous because of a lack of separation from liberalism, then the emerging church movement is even more dangerous because it does not believe in separation in any sense of the word. (it's the old "sitting around the bar and talking about Jesus" idea)

In an article that I recently read on the emerging church movement, the following people either refused to take a stand or else were very confused about the doctrine of salvation:

- ***Tony Campolo*** believes we are saved only through Jesus but does not want to say anyone else is lost if they don't believe in Jesus.

- ***Brian McLaren*** doesn't think we can "prognosticate the eternal destiny" of anyone.

• ***C.S. Lewis*** wrote in one of his novels about a soldier who served a false god but was accepted nonetheless by Aslan, who represents Christ.

To put it in a nutshell, the emerging church movement is teaching our people not to stand for anything and to question everything.

This type of mentality will water down and eventually destroy your church!

Prosperity Gospel

THE PROSPERITY GOSPEL teaches that God desires the material, spiritual, and physical prosperity of his people. To become prosperous, all one has to do is believe, receive, and act upon God's promises.

This is obviously false, as evidenced by the lives of Job, the apostles, and even Jesus himself.

So, prosperity preachers are clearly mixed up on what constitutes the abundant Christian life, but how does this qualify them as a cult?

The leading proponents of the prosperity gospel do not believe in preaching repentance and sometimes shun away from the sin issue altogether:

'Sin is any act or thought that robs myself or another human being of his or her self-esteem"(Schuller, Self-Esteem, p. 14).

"And what is 'hell'? It is the loss of pride that naturally follows separation from God—the ultimate and unfailing source of our soul's sense of self-respect. 'My God, my God, why hast thou forsaken me?' was Christ's encounter with hell. In that 'hellish' death our Lord experienced the ultimate horror—humiliation, shame, and loss of pride as a human being. A person is in hell when he has lost his self-esteem. Can you imagine any condition more tragic than to live life and eternity in shame?" (Schuller, Self-Esteem, pp. 14-15,93).

"The Cross sanctifies the ego trip. For the Cross protected our Lord's perfect self-esteem from turning into sinful pride" (Schuller, Self-Esteem, p. 75).

"Jesus never called a person a sinner. ... Rather he reserved his righteous rebuke for those who used their religious authority to generate guilt and caused people to lose their ability to taste and enjoy their right to dignity..." (Schuller, Self-Esteem, pp. 100,126).

A Few Final Thoughts

We can be encouraged by the truth that whatever is built upon Christ will last. (2 Timothy 2:15-19; 1 Corinthians 3:11) We can rest in knowing that the safety of the Lord's church and His Word is not entirely up to us.

Yet, we are still responsible for maintaining the purity of doctrine and practice.

What must we do in these last days to combat cults? (2 Timothy 4:1-4)

Teach your family the truth. (Deuteronomy 6:1-9) The home is the basic unit of society. What are you allowing to be taught in your home?

The average child spends roughly about 13,000 hours from kindergarten through High School in an academic environment designed to teach humanistic principles.

The same children (on average) are bombarded with 13,800 hours of television during this same 12-year period. The average viewer will ingest approximately 26 murders and hundreds of sexual innuendoes as well as actual sexual acts portrayed in a week. These are the most impressionable years of a person's life.

It only takes one generation to lose our children. (Joshua 24:31; Judges 2:10)

Teach the church. (2 Timothy 4:2-4) It is the responsibility of the Man of God to protect his flock. (Jeremiah 23:1-4)

Teach ourselves. (Proverbs 19:27) Never let yourself become blinded by charisma, education, looks, oratory ability, or anything else.

If what is being taught is not directly from the Word of God, cease hearing it. Remember, false teaching will only lead to deeper sin - no matter how good it sounds. (2 Timothy 2:16)

Appendix A - Korean Superstitions

South Korea has a variety of religions, which are practiced by more than half the population. The most common religions are Buddhism, Protestant Christianity, Catholicism, and Shamanism. Statistically speaking, 42.2 percent, or 17 million Koreans, confessed to belonging to an organized religious group. There are 8 million Buddhists, 6.5 million Protestants, 1.9 million Confucianists, and 500,000 Shamanists.

Each religion is unique and has its own teachings and practices. Also, most of the main religions came to Korea from other countries. Since their entry, 300 new religions and branches of the main religions have been formed.

Religion has a vital role in South Korean society. These roles start from the country's early development to its current thoughts, behavior, physical appearances, education, and followers of the beliefs.

Today, in South Korea, religion has developed into a complex and important part of society. This is evidenced by the religious temples, statues, and symbols located in the region.

Many people in South Korea are religious. It is a huge part of their culture. Spiritual practices and ceremonies are performed regularly and take up a significant part of one's time. The various religions also fight for human rights, provide social services, and even build and operate schools and colleges.

It is fair to say life in South Korea would not be the same without religion.

Tangun

Although Koreans have many beliefs about death and the afterlife, ***many*** also believe in a myth about how the civilization was started. This myth is called Tan-gun.

Tan-gun is a myth about a bear and a tiger that wished to become human.

The son of Heaven's supreme deity, Prince Hwanung, tells the bear and tiger that if they can stay in a dark cave for 100 days and only eat garlic and mugwort, they will become human.

The bear survived the ordeal; however, the tiger did not. The bear turned into a beautiful woman, married King Hwanung, and gave birth to the child Tan-gun.

Tan-gun later established the Choson kingdom in 2333 B.C. Tan-gun is said to be the father of the Korean civilization.

The true origin of the Korean people is not easily explained. However, since historical records show that Ko Choson (Old Choson), was the first Korean kingdom, it can be taken as the origin of the Korean people.

The Tan-gun myth describes the life of Ko Choson's heroic founder. Thus, Tan-gun is a historical person who lived during a specific stage of Korea's history. To the extent that his memory remains within the national consciousness, he can be considered an ancestor of the Korean people.

The Korean people have, throughout their history, constantly been threatened by the tremendous military might of neighboring nations such as China, Manchuria, or Mongolia.

In this precarious position, some Koreans have found strength in their sense of being unique people descended from Tan-gun.

The ancient records that referred to Tan-gun were lost in the chaos of frequent wars and invasions. During the Three Kingdoms period, when Koguryo, Paekche, and Shila vied for supremacy, the kingdoms found it challenging to promote the idea of a united people.

Yet in the aftermath of Shilla's unification of the Three Kingdoms in 668, Koreans' sense of themselves as a people was evident as Shilla joined forces with the former subjects of Koguryo and Paekche to drive away the Chinese Tang forces.

Other Superstitions

Many superstitions are believed by the Koreans.[31]

- If you whistle at night, then a snake will enter your house.

- If you wet your bed, you must ask your neighbors for salt.

- If you throw your baby tooth over the roof of your house, your adult tooth will grow straight.

- If you are a girl and you hold your chopsticks too close to the tip, it will take you a long time to get married.

- The number 4 is unlucky, so there are fewer buildings with a fourth level. Instead, the fourth floor is marked with an "F" or skipped altogether. Few people desire to live on the fourth floor of an apartment building.

• Names should never be written in red, as this is a sign of death when it is done in the family records. If a name is written in red, the person may die.

Of course, superstition is illogical. For example:

• If you live in Ireland (a country with no snakes) and whistle at night, what will enter your house? Maybe a leprechaun?

• If your neighbor has no salt, will rice be a suitable substitute?

• If you live in an apartment building (usually 15 or more floors high), are you destined to live with crooked teeth?

• If you are a guy and don't want to rush into marriage, do you look for a girl who holds her chopsticks close to the end?

• Does a child live in constant danger when he turns four years old?

• Are there special rules for people with a "red deficiency" in their eyesight?

Superstition is also unbiblical since it leads to bondage and fear (2 Timothy 1:7; Galatians 5:1; 2 Peter 2:20)

Proverbs 3:25 *Be not afraid of sudden fear, neither of the desolation of the wicked, when it cometh.*

Appendix B - Church of God World Mission Society

I. **Brief Background:**

    A. An Sang Hong (◇◇◇), born to Buddhist parents in 1918 in South Korea, joined the Seventh Day Adventists in 1947. He was baptized in 1948 to preach. He set up his own church in 1964. He was divorced and remarried several times. He predicted the Second Coming of Christ would occur in 1967, and then 1988. Apparently he himself did not believe he was Christ.[32]

    B. After An's death in 1985, the church transformed. At present, the group has an aggressive proselytization emphasis.

    C. The current leader is Kim Joo-Cheol (◇◇◇). The group claims to have as many as 400,000 members worldwide in 70 countries.[33] They claim to have 300 branch churches as of 1985.[34], and as of 2007, 400 churches in Korea.[35]

    D. Chung Gil Cha (◇◇◇), a former lover of An Sang Hong, is the charismatic matriarch of the church, who claims to be the incarnation of God as Mother Jerusalem.[36]

I. **Beliefs and Refutation:**

THEOLOGY

1. There is a "heavenly family" that corresponds to the human family.

"**Heb. 8:5** ◇They serve at a sanctuary that is a copy and shadow of what is in heaven.◇

"All of the earthly systems are a copy and a shadow of what is in heaven. The family system is the same. Christ Ahnsahnghong revealed to us the existence of the heavenly Mother by teaching us about the heavenly family system through the earthly family system.

"Everything within the spiritual world is reflected on this earth. In other words, everything on the earth is a shadow, and the things in heaven are the realities of what is on earth."[37]

** **The Tabernacle is a shadow of the Tabernacle in Heaven, but the Bible does not say that everything is.**

1. An Sang Hong is God the Father

"The God in heaven is our God the Father. Just as we have a physical father on this earth, we have a spiritual Father in heaven. He is God the Father, Ahnsahnghong." [38]

1. **An Sang Hong is the second return of Christ.**

The WMSCOG claims that An Sang Hong ascended into heaven in 1985.[39] Rather, he is buried in the ground in South Gyeong-sang Province, Yang-san City, Sang-buk-myeon, Oe-seok-ri 8-1.[40]

1. An Sang Hong is the Holy Spirit.

**** It is really hard to keep their beliefs straight. They believe the name of God (Elohim) in the present age is An Sang Hong, as he is the Holy Spirit, as distinguished from God the Father in the Old Testament, and Jesus the Son in the New Testament. So there is a real lack of coherence on <u>which</u> person of the Trinity An Sang Hong is supposed to be.**

1. **We become children of this "Heavenly Father" by keeping the Sabbath and the Passover.**

"**Matt. 12:46** ◇While Jesus was still talking to the crowd, his mother and brothers stood outside, wanting to speak to him. Someone told him, "Your mother and brothers are standing outside, wanting to speak to you." He replied to him, "Who is my mother, and who are my brothers?" Pointing to his disciples, he said, "Here are my mother and my brothers. For whoever does the will of my Father in heaven is my brother and sister and mother."◇

"Here, we can find the words "brothers" and "sisters." Just as we have physical brothers and sisters, we have spiritual brothers and sisters. God's children, who call upon the God in heaven as "Father," must follow the will of the heavenly Father. In the Church of God, the children of the heavenly Father keep the Sabbath, the Passover, and all of the other truths, according to the will of the Father in heaven. The Church of God follows the teachings of Christ Ahnsahnghong, and we are brothers and sisters."[41]

** **Note that Matthew 12:46 also says whoever does the will of God is "mother", the same as brother and sister. WMSCOG reserves "mother" for one person, Chung Gil Cha. The correct interpretation of the passage is that Jesus was teaching those who follow Him are closer than family members. The will of God for believers today is not keeping the Sabbath and the Passover, as will be shown later.**

1. **There is a Heavenly Mother, Chung Gil Cha, a lover of An Sang Hong, Mother Jerusalem.**
   a. **The mother of us all.**

"We have studied that there exists a God the Father, and His children, in the heavenly family. Then, who is left? It's Mother.

"**Gal. 4:25-26** ◇Now Hagar stands for Mount Sinai in Arabia and corresponds to the present city of Jerusalem, because she is in slavery with her children. But the Jerusalem that is above is free, and she is our mother.◇

"In this verse we can find the words "our mother." "Our" refers to the children who believe in God. This verse reveals that there exists a heavenly Mother to the children who will be saved."[42]

*** This is not referring to a human being, but the church as a symbol of the New Testament. In context, there is contrast made between the covenant of law given on Sinai (4:24-25); and the New Testament. "Jerusalem which is above" is the New Jerusalem (Revelation 21:2, 9-10), which will "descend out of heaven from God". It is a future literal city, complete with foundations, walls, gates, and measurements, into which people may enter (Revelation 21:11-27). It makes reference to the 12 tribes of Israel, and the 12 apostles; thus it encompasses both Israel and the church. The "bride, the Lamb's wife" is the church (Ephesians 5:25-27; 2 Corinthians 11:2; John 3:29).*

a. God made male and female in his image.

"**Gen. 1:26-27** ◇Then God said, "Let us make man in our image, in our likeness,"...So God created man in his own image, in the image of God he created him; male and female he created them.◇

"Both males and females were created in the image of God, and thus it is clear that God has two images: a male image and a female image. When God said, "Let us make man in our image," God used the word "us"—a plural term—instead of using "me." We come to understand that not one God, but two Gods—a Father and a Mother—worked together during the Creation. Such plural terms are used to describe God in Genesis chapter 11, also."

*** God created "adam" (and by extension, mankind) in His image. He designed mankind to be both male and female, but this does not imply that God is part female. Never in the Bible is God mentioned as a woman. The plural words for God (elohim) refer to His trinity.*

a. The Spirit and the Bride

154

"**Rev. 22:17** ◇The Spirit and the bride say, "Come!" And let him who hears say, "Come!" Whoever is thirsty, let him come; and whoever wishes, let him take the free gift of the water of life.◇

"For our salvation, God always referred to Himself as "us," and then Elohim God appeared—as the Holy Spirit and the Bride—to give us the water of life. In the first book of Timothy, it is written that God alone is immortal and lives in unapproachable light (1 Tim. 6:16). Thus, only the Spirit and the Bride—the Second Coming Christ, Ahnsahnghong, and the New Jerusalem Mother—are immortal and only They have life. Nevertheless, some people boast that they, also, have the power to give life. The people who make such assumptions are greatly mistaken. The Bible says that no one can have life until he or she eats the flesh of the Son of Man and drinks His blood (John 6:53), and Jesus said, "Follow me, and let the dead bury their own dead" (Matt. 8:22). Mere human beings, such as ourselves, cannot say that we are alive.

"There is no life in us, so we must go to God—Christ Ahnsahnghong and Mother—if we want to receive eternal life and salvation, because They are the only ones who have life. In order to give the everlasting water of life to mortal beings, God came down to this earth in this last age as the Holy Spirit, Ahnsahnghong, and the Bride, the New Jerusalem Mother. People who pervert or deny this Biblical teaching will never be able to enter the kingdom of heaven."[43]

*** The Spirit is the Holy Spirit, not An Sang Hong. The bride is the church, as pointed out earlier. The Holy Spirit convicts people of the need for salvation (John 16:8-11); and He uses the church to call people to salvation (Acts 1:8).*

*** There is no Biblical teaching that God would come down as An Sang Hong, and as a Bride.*

*** Where we see the "Queen of Heaven" in the Bible, it is a reference to a pagan idol (Jeremiah 7:18).*

ESCHATOLOGY

1. An Sang Hong is Jesus' Second Return

"The Bible prophesies that Jesus will come on a cloud, for a second time, in order to restore the lost truth and to lead the children of

God into the kingdom of heaven. When Jesus came two thousand years ago, He fulfilled the prophecy of the book of Daniel by "coming with the clouds of heaven" (Dan. 7:13-14). Actually, Jesus came as a man, in the flesh. Jesus is prophesied to come a second time on the clouds of heaven, meaning that He will come as a man, in the flesh, again."[44]

*** Actually, the prophecy in Daniel 7:13-14 refers to Christ's second coming, not his first. They are right to believe that Jesus will come again in the flesh, but in literal clouds, not as a reincarnation. Also, Jesus will come "with the clouds", not "on a cloud".*

1. He would return in "clouds" – that is "people", thus as a human being.

"Dan. 7:13-14 ◈In my vision at night I looked, and there before me was one like a son of man, coming with the clouds of heaven. He approached the Ancient of Days and was led into his presence. He was given authority, glory and sovereign power; all peoples, nations and men of every language worshiped him. His dominion is an everlasting dominion that will not pass away, and his kingdom is one that will never be destroyed.◈

"Jesus did not come on the visible clouds of heaven. Instead, He was born as a baby through the body of Mary. Some argue that the above prophecy is concerning Jesus' second coming. Daniel's prophecy is speaking of Jesus' first coming, undoubtedly, because the prophecy states, "He was given authority, glory and sovereign power [a kingdom, KJV]; all peoples, nations and men of every language worshiped him." Matthew and Luke disclosed that, in His first coming, Jesus had been given all authority, in heaven and on earth, as well as a kingdom. (Matthew 28:18; Luke 22:29)"[45]

*** This is a figurative interpretation. If they do not take this prophecy literally, why should we take any eschatological prophecy literally? The prophecies of Daniel 7:13-14 do not match Christ's first coming. He was not universally worshiped, neither did He set up a kingdom. Matthew 28:18 speaks of His authority that He had as the Son of God; and Luke 22:29 speaks of the kingdom that was "appointed" but not yet realized – that is the millennial kingdom in which He would rule over Israel. None of this happened during Christ's first coming.*

*** "Clouds" means "clouds". Acts 1:9 tells us that a cloud received Jesus, obviously not a reference to people. He is coming again "in like manner" (Acts 1:11). It would be "this same Jesus", not a Korean reincarnation.*

*** Also note than when Christ returns, "every eye shall see Him" (Revelation 1:7). Has everyone seen An Sang Hong?*

"In the above expressions [Hebrews 12:1; Jude 12) —"a great cloud of witnesses," and, "clouds without rain, blown along by the wind"—the clouds represent people, wearing the flesh. Since the Bible calls false prophets "clouds without rain," whom do "clouds with rain" represent? Those "with rain" are the true prophets, aren't they?

"The water within the clouds represents the water of life. (Zech. 14:8; John 7:37-39; 2 Pet. 2:17)

"Springs without water" and "mists driven by a storm" indicate false Christians. As you know, "mists" are "clouds without rain" (Jude 1:12). The waters that have not been vaporized represent all human beings, everyone in the flesh.

"Since the waters represent "peoples," (Revelation 17:15) whom do the clouds stand for? Clouds are suspended in the air, visible collections of water particles that have been vaporized by solar heat.

Thus, clouds represent the people who have been born again through the Holy Spirit. Jesus' coming in a cloud means His coming in the flesh."[46]

*** "Cloud" is obviously figurative in Hebrews 12:1 and Jude 12, in contrast to Daniel 7:13-14 and Acts 1:9-11. If it means "people", then Hebrews 12:1 should read, "We also are compassed about by so great a <u>people</u> of witnesses..." In Jude, do "trees" also represent people? This is extremely stretched symbolism. Also, it is a confusing metaphor. Is it the clouds or the water itself that is supposed to represent "people"?*

1. He is from the "east".

"Isa. 24:15-16 ◇Therefore in the east give glory to the LORD; exalt the name of the LORD, the God of Israel, in the islands of the sea. From the ends of the earth we hear singing: "Glory to the Righteous One."◇

"The above prophecy reveals that God's chosen people will give glory and praise to the God in the east. When we read this chapter from the first verse, it is clear that this prophecy is concerning the last day—the last day when God will ruin the earth's face and will burn up all of the inhabitants. When God banishes all of the gaiety form the earth, a certain group of people will shout for joy and will give glory to God, meaning that God would guide His chosen people on the last day, from the east.

"Then, where is "the east"? First, we have to know the point of origin. Isaiah prophesied from the country of Israel. Thus, "the east" must be a land east of Israel: Asia. Among the countries in Asia, which country is located towards the east, "at the ends of the earth"? Russia is to the north, India is south, and China is Central Asia. Even Japan, though located in the east, is not a land at the ends of the earth—it is in the middle of the sea.

"It is only Korea that is located in the east, at the ends of the earth. Thus, the Second Coming Christ is prophesied to come from Korea, in the east, at the ends of the earth. In accordance with the prophecy, Christ Ahnsahnghong came from Korea."[47]

*** In context, it is a command for the whole earth to glorify God. Also, it is not good hermeneutics to superimpose "the uttermost part of the earth" (vs 16) on "the east" [KJV – "the fires"] (vs 15).*

*** "Only Korea is located in the east"? Why not Japan? The verse even mentioned the "islands". If it is the uttermost part, why not Russia's Sakhalin Peninsula?*

*** Also, it is only a command to praise God; there is certainly no implied promise that Christ would come from the east.*

"Isa. 41:2 ◇"Who has stirred up one from the east, calling him in righteousness to his service? He hands nations over to him and subdues kings before him..."◇

The above verse states that God "has stirred up one from the east." Since it is prophesied that kings are subdued before "the one," he must be a man of great power. Then, who is "the one"? If we read the same chapter, beginning in verse four, we can come to know who "the one" is.

Isa. 41:4 ◇"Who has done this and carried it through, calling forth the generations from the beginning? I, the LORD—with the first of them and with the last—I am he."◇

The one whom God "has stirred up" is God, Himself. This prophecy means that God Himself will come in the flesh, from the east. "The one" who came in fulfillment of this prophecy is God Ahnsahnghong.

In chapter 46 of the same book, Isaiah, it is written:

Isa. 46:11 ◇From the east I summon a bird of prey; from a far-off land, a man to fulfill my purpose. What I have said, that will I bring about; what I have planned, that will I do.◇

The prophet Isaiah recorded again about "the one" who would arise from the east, from a far-off land. In the Bible, a bird of prey—or, an eagle—represents God (Deut. 32:11; Ex. 19:4). Since this "bird of prey" coming from the east is described as a man who would fulfill God's purpose, it is very clear that God, Himself, would come from the east as a man, in the flesh. The one who fulfilled this prophecy is God Ahnsahnghong."[48]

*** The "one" who God stirs up was Cyrus the king of Persia, who is mentioned by name in Isaiah 44:28; 45:1. What God "hath wrought and done" in 41:4 was to "raise up the righteous man from the east". The "Who?" questions are parallel. It does not say that God was the man.*

*** Who was the one that was raised up from the north (Isaiah 41:25)? Doesn't that mean that God would come in the flesh from Russia, according to this system of "interpretation"?*

*** Apparently they found any reference to the word "east" in the Bible that was favorable, and tried to apply it to An Sang Hong. Why are the "kings of the east" (Revelation 16:12) not a reference to Korea?*

1. **His "new name" is An Sang Hong.**
2. **His ministry began in 1948 (fig tree), at the age of 30.**

"Through the parable of the fig tree (Matthew 24:32-34), Jesus revealed that He would come for the second time in 1948, when Israel—represented as the fig tree—would gain its independence. Ahnsahnghong came in 1948 according to the prophecy of the fig tree, so the Church of God believes in Him as the Second Coming Christ."[49]

*** The fig tree can represent Israel, but that doesn't seem to be what is in view here. Rather, the plain interpretation is that, as we can see the fig tree's fruit and know summer is near, so when we see the things described in Matthew 24, we know the end is near.*

*** If An Sang Hong really were Christ's return, then why haven't
we seen the signs in Matthew 24? Why hasn't he set up his
kingdom? Also, many people were baptized in 1948, not just An
Sang Hong.*

"Rom. 11:26 ◇And so all Israel will be saved, as it is written: "The
deliverer will come from Zion; he will turn godlessness away from
Jacob."◇

"Ahnsahnghong, the Second Coming Jesus, came from Zion in
1948, as had been prophesied in the parable of the fig tree. Now He
is calling you. Will you let Him stand at your door, or will you open
the door and receive Him?"[50]

*** An Sang Hong did not come from Zion, but from Korea. But
even if so, why hasn't all Israel been saved? If An did not do this, he
failed to fulfill the prophecy.*

1. He would minister for 37 years, as David ruled for 40, and Christ
    as the successor of David would need to minister an additional 37
    years besides the 3 of His "first coming".

*** No Scriptural support for this.*

1. They also seem to believe in a coming eschatological event. They
    seem to believe in a "third coming", which would be the result of
    things not going as planned with An Sang Hong's life (i.e., he died,
    and didn't ascend).

We know the end of the world is near, although we can't set a date.
[51]

SOTERIOLOGY

There is a heavy emphasis on keeping all the laws. This legalism is almost identical to that of the Seventh Day Adventists; with the addition of the Passover.

**** *If one keeps the ceremonial law, he is a debtor to the whole law (Galatians 5:3). Why don't they sacrifice animals also?***

1. **Salvation is through keeping the Passover (Lord's Supper) every year.**

"Actually, no one can be said to be "saved" without knowing about the Passover."[52]

a. **We must eat Christ's flesh and blood to be saved.**

"Then, through what truth can we receive the right to become God's children? How can we inherit the flesh and blood of our heavenly Father?

"Matt. 26:26-28 ◇While they were eating, Jesus took bread, gave thanks and broke it, and gave it to his disciples, saying, "Take and eat; this is my body." Then he took the cup, gave thanks and offered it to them, saying, "Drink from it, all of you. This is my blood of the covenant, which is poured out for many for the forgiveness of sins.◇

*** As shown above, the Passover bread is Jesus' body, His flesh, and the Passover wine is Jesus' blood. By eating and drinking the bread and wine of the Passover, we can receive God's flesh and blood and become God's children."*[53]

*** Luke 22:20 makes it clear that the Lord's Supper was instituted "after supper", that is, after the Passover meal was finished. Certainly the two are not the same, as the very elements are different.*

*** The bread and wine were symbols of Christ's body and blood, which would be sacrificed on the cross the next day.*

Then, how will God grant us eternal life? God gives us salvation through the blood of Christ (1 Cor. 5:7), represented, during the time of the Exodus, by the blood of the Passover lamb."[54]

*** "Christ our Passover" is the fulfillment of the Passover, not a command to keep the Passover.*

"Jesus promised that the bread of the Passover was His flesh, and that the wine of the Passover was His blood. (John 6:53-55)

"The reason why we want to receive the flesh and blood of Jesus—given to us through the Passover—is because Jesus, who is life, promised that when we eat His flesh and drink His blood, we will live forever.

"Since Jesus said, "unless you eat the flesh of the Son of Man and drink his blood, you have no life in you" (John 6:53), how can we receive eternal life unless we celebrate the Passover?"[55]

*** This is obviously symbolic. Jesus' body and blood was still alive when He said that, so obviously He did not intend for them to literally eat Him. Rather, it is a symbol of partaking in Christ's death and resurrection.*

*** All holy days of the law were fulfilled and completed in Christ (Colossians 2:13-17). This includes Passover.*

a.   Passover keeping was stopped by Constantine.

"The Passover was abolished at the Council of Nicaea in A.D. 325. At that time, the Passover completely disappeared from the world. Who on earth can have eternal life as the truth of life was abolished? Therefore, Jesus said that He would come a second time to restore the Passover."[56]

*** At another place, they claim that the Passover was abolished in A.D. 167. Which is right? When did Jesus say He would come to restore the Passover?*

*** Incidentally, the WMSCOG does not celebrate the feast of Firstfruits on the day God prescribed in the Jewish calendar, but substitutes Resurrection day instead.[57] They claim the Feast of Trumpets symbolize the Advent Movement led by William Miller from 1833 to 1844. They accept the 7th Day Adventist teaching that Christ entered into the Most Holy Place on October 22, 1844.[58] Why pick and choose what must be literal?*

a.   Only the Church of God keeps the Passover.

"The Church of God is the only church in the world that celebrates the Passover of the new covenant on the fourteenth day of the first month—by sacred year—as was written in the Bible (Lev. 23:4). The Church of God can celebrate the Passover because the Second Coming Christ, Ahnsahnghong, has restored the Passover that Jesus established two thousand years ago."[59]

*** Actually, there are other religious groups that still celebrate Passover, including the Orthodox Jews.**

1. **The Sabbath must be kept.**
   a. *The Sabbath is Saturday*

"The Church of God, that has received the Second Coming Christ Ahnsahnghong, keeps the Sabbath on Saturday, according to the Bible. The seventh-day Sabbath is the day on which God rested from creating the heavens and the earth. Most Christians are mistaken as to what day the seventh-day Sabbath is, believing it to be Sunday, even though the Bible testifies that the Sabbath is Saturday. And they do not keep the Sabbath day, being bound to their customs, even though they realize that the Sabbath is actually Saturday." [60]

*** It is true that the Sabbath is Saturday; however, Colossians 2:16-17 makes it clear that the Sabbath is done away; of course it is not mentioned in the WMSCOG materials. Why do they judge for not keeping a day?**

a. **The Sabbath was changed to Sunday by Constantine and the Catholics.**

"Sunday service, a worldwide tradition, is another church doctrine tied to sun-worship. Sunday is "the day of the sun," on which the Romans worshiped the sun god. Constantine, a Roman emperor, instituted Sunday as the day of rest and worship in 321 A.D., as follows:

"All judges, city-people and craftsmen shall rest on the venerable day of the Sun. But countrymen may without hindrance attend to agriculture, since it often happens that this is the most suitable day for sowing grain or planting vines, so that the opportunity afforded by divine providence may not be lost, for the right season is short." (7 March 321) "[61]

What Constantine may have done makes no difference to Colossians 2:16-17. Support for Sunday worship can be found in John 20:1, 19, 26; Acts 1; 1 Corinthians 16:1-2; Revelation 1:10.

1. Baptism is also necessary for salvation.

"We cannot have life when we are still filled with sin. In order to receive eternal life, our sins must be disposed of. Baptism is the first step we can take toward salvation. Through this gracious regulation of God, our sins are cleansed and we are atoned.

"Therefore, the Church of God performs baptism, according to the teaching of the Second Coming Christ Ahnsahnghong."[62]

They use Acts 8:36-37; but in that passage it can easily be seen that the eunuch was required to believe before baptism. They also use Acts 16:30-33; and in that passage also it is clear that only faith is necessary for salvation.

"Jesus said, "No one can enter the kingdom of God unless he is born of water and the Spirit." To be "born again" means to be born a second time—being born of the Spirit (John 3:1-8). As one's name is recorded in the census when he is born, so is one's name written in the book of life after he is born again of the Spirit. Therefore, when someone is baptized, his name is written in the Church's book of life, and most importantly, is also written in the book of life in heaven."[63]

The discovery of truth by analogy (of the census) is very weak. The water described in this passage is physical birth, as Nicodemus himself hinted at.

1. *Women wearing head coverings during worship is also necessary for salvation.*

"All of the women of the Church of God wear veils during worship services, according to the teachings of the Second Coming Christ Ahnsahnghong. By wearing veils, they can worship God with a godly mind. Men do not cover their heads during worship services.

"God gave us this veil regulation as a sign representing God's authority. Even though this regulation seems minor, it cannot be neglected. None of God's commands were instituted meaninglessly. All of the regulations were given to God's people because they are necessary for our salvation and allow us to enter the kingdom of God."[64]

*** In the context of 1 Corinthians 11:1-16, the covering is the woman's hair (vs 15). It is not given as a requirement for salvation.**

*** The Bible teaches salvation by grace through faith without works (Ephesians 2:8-9; Galatians 2:16, etc.). This heresy teaches salvation by the works of the law.**

HERMENEUTICS

1. **There are three dispensations; the Old Testament (Father - Jehovah); New Testament (Son - Jesus); and the church age (Spirit – An Sang Hong).**

Matt. 28:19 ◇"Therefore go and make disciples of all nations, baptizing them in the name of the Father and of the Son and of the Holy Spirit, and teaching them to obey everything I have commanded you. And surely I am with you always, to the very end of the age."◇

"As is commonly known, the name of the Father is "Jehovah," and the name of the Son is "Jesus." Baptism is the first step that we can take towards becoming a child of God, and to be baptized correctly, we must first know the name of the Father, the name of the Son, and the name of the Holy Spirit.[65]

*** The "name of the Father..." is not intended to represent a proper name, but is rather a Trinitarian formula showing Father, Son, and Holy Spirit. By name is meant their authority, and identification with them.**

a. Salvation in the Old Testament was through the name of Jehovah.

"Once we come to understand the time limitations of each age, it is very easy for us to understand how each age affected the salvation of God's people. In the age of the Father, people were the witnesses of Jehovah (Isa. 43:10), they prayed in the name of Jehovah, and salvation was promised only through the name of Jehovah (Joel 2:32).[66]

** *In Isaiah 43:10, it is clear that there is no one to be after Jehovah; thus that would eliminate a Jesus or An Sang Hong separate from the name of Jehovah.*

** *Joel 2:32 is a reference to Pentecost, and also to Christ's second coming, showing that Jehovah's name is used in both.*

a. Salvation in the New Testament was through the name of Jesus.

"The Bible states that in the age of the Father there was no Savior apart from Jehovah, and that in the age of the Son there was no Savior apart from Jesus.

"Acts 4:11-12 ◈"He is 'the stone you builders rejected, which has become the capstone.' Salvation is found in no one else, for there is no other name under heaven given to men by which we must be saved."◈

When God gave the names of Jehovah and Jesus to the people, He did not explain that each of these Savior's names would only be used for a specific time period or age. Thus, many people have become confused, believing that the Bible contradicts itself."[67]

** *They are not exclusive titles. Jesus means "Jehovah saves". Of course are confused by the WMSCOG's claims, because they are not found in Scripture.*

"Once the age of the Son had begun, how did the people, who were to receive salvation, act? Did they insist on praying in the name of Jehovah as the witnesses of Jehovah, believing that they could only be saved through the name of Jehovah? Jesus' disciples became the witnesses of Jesus (Acts 1:6), they prayed in the name of Jesus (John 16:24), and they received salvation only by believing the name of Jesus (Rom. 10:9).[68]

a. Salvation in the present age is through the name of the Holy Spirit (An Sang Hong).

"Now we are living in the age of the Holy Spirit. Thus, God has given us a new name of the Savior.

"Rev. 3:12 ◇"Him who overcomes I will make a pillar in the temple of my God. Never again will he leave it. I will write on him the name of my God and the name of the city of my God, the new Jerusalem, which is coming down out of heaven from my God; and I will also write on him my new name."◇

"A "white stone with a new name written on it" is mentioned in the above verse [Revelation 2:17]. In this instance, the stone represents Jesus (1 Pet. 2:4), meaning that a new name other than the name of Jesus would be given to the people of that age.

"Just as salvation was withheld from those who were stuck on the name of Jehovah and failed to receive Jesus as their Savior in the age of the Son (Rom. 15:4), salvation will never be given to those who are stuck on the name of Jesus in this age.

"...We need to understand God's providence of salvation—His allowing a different Savior's name for each age—and we need to accept Christ Ahnsahnghong, the Savior's name in this age of the Holy Spirit, Jesus' new name."[69]

*** The stone doesn't necessarily represent Jesus, as in 1 Peter 2:4-5, stones also represent believers. As far as a new name, how about "King of Kings and Lord of Lords" (Revelation 19:16)? That certainly is as good of a guess as "An Sang Hong".*

*** In any case, it never says that the name of Jesus will change, or that salvation will ever be exclusively through His "new name".*

*** Jesus Christ is the same yesterday, and today and forever (Hebrews 13:8).*

*** The Holy Spirit, which was promised (John 14:16-17; 16:13), would come "not many days hence" (Acts 1:5). Why would the Holy Spirit need to come again after Pentecost?*

BIBLIOLOGY

1. **The Bible can only be understood through An Sang Hong and the Church of God.**

"Our standard of judgment must be the Bible, not the opinions of men. The Church of God, established by Christ Ahnsahnghong, follows only the teachings of the Bible, and can thus be easily recognized as the true Church."[70]

*** They profess to follow only the Bible; but as seen, they do not interpret the Bible literally and contextually. Instead, they rely upon the interpretations of An Sang Hong and Chung Gil Cha. They say that no one could understand the Bible fully without being initiate.*

ANTHROPOLOGY

1. **Men are angels who sinned in heaven.**

"Christ Ahnsahnghong came to the earth, established the Church of God, and taught us that all men are angels who have come to the earth after sinning in heaven. He let us know how valuable we are and revealed to us the true purpose of our lives."[71]

*** The Bible does not teach this at all; but rather teaches that God created Adam from dust, and that we reproduce after our kind.*

Page of 165

---

[1] Some 35,000 couples officiated over by Sun Myung Moon (b. 1920) of the Holy Spirit Association for the Unification of World Christianity were married in the Olympic Stadium in Seoul, South Korea on 25 August 1995. (Guness Book of World Records)

[2] In Christ's case, His "preconceived theology" is right. Since He is the Truth, His thoughts were always right.

[3] Three important concepts in understanding Buddhism are *karma*, *samsara*, and *nirvana*.
Karma refers to the law of cause and effect in a person's life, reaping what one has sown. Buddhists believe that every person must go through a process of birth and rebirth until he reaches the state of *nirvana* in which he breaks this cycle. For a Buddhist, what one will be in the next life depends on one's actions in this present life. Unlike Hindus, Buddha believed that a person can break the rebirth cycle no matter what class he is born into.
Samsara or *transmigration*. The law of Samsara holds that everything is in a birth and rebirth cycle. Buddha taught that people do not have individual souls. The existence of an individual self or ego is an illusion. There is no eternal substance of a person, which goes through the rebirth cycle. What is it then that goes through the cycle if not the individual soul? What goes through the rebirth cycle is only a set of feelings, impressions, present moments, and the karma that is passed on.
Nirvana. The term means "the blowing out" of existence. Nirvana is not a place like heaven, but rather an eternal state of being. It is the state in which the law of karma and the rebirth cycle come to an end. It is the end of suffering; a state where there are no desires and the individual consciousness comes to an end. However, the Bible teaches that in the eternal state, we are fully conscious of our existence, whether that existence be in Heaven or Hell.

[4] Clark, Charles A., Religions of Old Korea; Christian Literature Society; pg 16

[5]http://www.buddhanet.net/e-learning/history/statistics.htm;
http://www.adherents.com/largecom/com_buddhist.html

[6] Clark, Charles A., Religions of Old Korea; Christian Literature Society; pg 27

[7] Doniger, Wendy; Encyclopedia of Wold Religions; Merriam-Webster Inc.; pg 162

[8] Clark, Charles A., Religions of Old Korea; Christian Literature Society; pg 28

[9] Ibid,; pg 29 - 25

[10] Ibid.; pg 40

[11] This god is referred to as Lord Maitreya in the USA and as Mi Dok (◇◇) in Korea.

[12] The *Analects*, also known as the *Sayings of Confucius*, is an ancient Chinese philosophical text composed of sayings and ideas attributed to Confucius and his contemporaries, traditionally believed to have been compiled by his followers. The consensus among scholars is that large portions of the text were composed during the Warring States period (475–221 BC), and that the work achieved its final form during the mid-Han dynasty[1] (206 BC – 220 AD). During the early Han, the *Analects* was merely considered to be a commentary on the Five Classics. However, by the dynasty's end the status of the *Analects* had grown to being among the central texts of Confucianism. (Wikipedia)

[13] The period takes its name from the Spring and Autumn Annals, a chronicle of the period whose authorship was traditionally attributed to Confucius.

[14] Much of the information in the section is adapted from <u>Religions of Korea</u> by Charles Allen Clark who was a missionary in Korea during the early 1900s and did extensive research in the area of ancient religions in Korea.

[15] In reality, they will play together, and function as friends, but may not call one another "friend".

[16] The term "Aryans" is often used to refer to a group of people who lived in ancient times, primarily in the Indus Valley, now parts of Pakistan and India. They are known for their contributions to the Vedic religion and Sanskrit language. However, the concept of Aryans as a distinct race has been debunked by modern scholars, who view it as a linguistic and cultural grouping rather than a racial one.

[17] Zoroastrianism is one of the world's oldest monotheistic religions, founded by Prophet Zoroaster in ancient Iran approximately 3500 years ago. It is based on the teachings of Zoroaster and emphasizes a dualistic cosmology of good and evil. Zoroastrianism was once the dominant religion of much of Greater Iran. As of 2007 the faith has dwindled to small numbers; some sources suggest that it is practiced by fewer than 200,000 worldwide, with its largest centers in India and Iran.

[18] Transcendental Meditation (TM) is a specific form of meditation introduced in 1955 by Maharishi Mahesh Yogi. It involves the use of a mantra and is often practiced for 15–20 minutes twice a day while sitting with eyes closed. The goal is to reduce stress and develop a deeper state of consciousness. It may be said to be both a form of meditation and a form of Hinduism. Their God (Brahma) is not the God of the Bible, but a god or essence that cannot be described.

Transcendental Meditation, often referred to as TM, is a specific form of silent mantra meditation developed by Maharishi Mahesh Yogi. Unlike many religions, it doesn't have a set of beliefs or dogma. The core belief is that regular practice of TM allows the mind to settle into a state of "restful alertness," which is thought to improve overall well-being and promote self-realization. In TM, God is within you; Christ was only a leader. There is no sin.

[19] The Vedas (1500—1200 B.C.) are considered to be divine in their origin. However, they present a worldview that is utterly opposed to a Biblical worldview, and both cannot be right at the same time.

[20] The Kaaba was a central place of worship for various tribes in the Arabian Peninsula. Before the advent of Islam, it housed numerous idols and deities. When Muhammad conquered Mecca in 630 A.D., he cleansed the Kaaba of its idols, rededicating it to the worship of Allah alone. Over the course of history, the Kaaba has undergone several reconstructions. These were necessitated by various

---

1.   https://en.wikipedia.org/wiki/Han_dynasty

factors, including damage from natural disasters and other significant events. The most recent major reconstruction, undertaken in 1996, was a crucial step to fortify its foundations and ensure its longevity."

[21] Cloud, David; Way of Life Encyclopedia; Article on Judaism

[22] It is difficult for scholars to reconstruct the daily workings and beliefs of Mithraism, as the rituals were highly secret and limited to initiated men only. Mithras was little more than a name until the massive documentation of Franz Cumont's *Texts and Illustrated Monuments Relating to the Mysteries of Mithra* was published in 1894-1900, followed by an English translation in 1903.Members would ascend through seven grades of initiation, each aligned with a symbol, and a god: 1) Corax: The Raven with Mercury; 2) Nymphus: The Bridegroom with Venus; 3) Miles: The Soldier with Mars; 4) Leo: The Lion with Jupiter; 5) Perses: The Persian with the Moon; 6) Heliodromus: The Runner of the Sun or the Messenger with the Sun; 7) Pater: The Father with Saturn. Archeological evidence suggests that initiations involved three ordeals that the initiate had to endure: heat, cold, and hunger. Since Father was the highest rank it is obviously one mentioned most frequently in inscriptions, but becoming a Lion was also seen to be very important. (http://en.wikipedia.org/wiki/Mithras#Religion)

[23] A henotheist is one who believes in the existence of many gods, but focuses primary on one particular god, or considers one particular god supreme over the other gods.

[24] (http://en.wikipedia.org/wiki/Gregory_the_Great

[25] http://www.newadvent.org/cathen/07674d.htm

[26] In actuality, Joseph Smith was shooting back at the mob in self-defense. No martyr would take this action.

[27] Mormons believe that God the Father, Jesus Christ, and the Holy Ghost are three distinct beings who form the Godhead. They also believe that God the Father was once a mortal human being who progressed to become God, and that human beings have the potential to progress similarly through obedience to God's commandments and eternal principles. This doctrine of eternal progression implies that as individuals progress towards perfection and godliness, they can eventually become gods themselves, creating the potential for many gods throughout eternity.

[28] According to LDS doctrine, the practice of using water instead of wine dates back to a revelation received by Joseph Smith in the early 19th century.

[29] The context of this statement by the Mormons is not that God became a man (as in Jesus Christ) but that a man became God.

[30] Also called the "emergent" church. Some of the churches that hold to this philosophy refer to themselves as such.

[31] Most of these are things that I have personally heard or seen in my experience living in Korea since the early eighties (1983 to be exact). Though not all people believe these superstitions, they are fairly well-known by most Koreans.

[32]Cult Watch – The World Mission Society Church of God","
ahnsahnghong.tripod.com/index.html

[33]Instinct to Escape Disasters, But Inevitable Reality", http://english.watv.org/who/"
truth.html

[34]About Church of God", http://english.watv.org/who/index.html"

[35]Press Release", http://english.watv.org/who/press.html"

[36] Incidentally, the WMSCOG website never gives her name, though they talk about
the "Heavenly Mother" extensively.

[37] http://text.watv.org/english/truth/view.html?idx=251

[38] http://text.watv.org/english/truth/view.html?idx=254

[39] See their timeline of history.

[40]◇◇ ◇◇ ◇◇ ◇◇◇◇ ◇◇◇ ◇◇◇ ◇◇◇ 8-1 ◇◇◇◇◇◇. ◇◇ ◇◇ ◇
◇◇◇◇◇◇ ◇◇ ◇◇◇◇◇◇ ◇◇ ◇◇◇ ◇◇ ◇◇◇◇◇◇◇ ◇◇ ◇◇. ◇◇◇◇
◇◇◇ ◇◇◇ ◇◇ ◇◇◇ ◇◇◇ ◇◇◇◇ ◇◇ ◇◇ ◇◇ ◇◇◇ ◇ ◇◇◇ ◇◇◇. -
http://www.jesustv.com.au/news/news_detail.html?sort=102&seq=902

[41] http://text.watv.org/english/truth/view.html?idx=255

[42] http://text.watv.org/english/truth/view.html?idx=256

[43]Elohim Will Appear In His Own Time", http://text.watv.org/english/truth/"
view.html?idx=603

[44]Clouds and Flesh", http://text.watv.org/english/truth/view.html?idx=303"

[45]Jesus, Who Came With the Clouds", http://text.watv.org/english/truth/"
view.html?idx=306

[46]Cloud" Means "Flesh"", http://text.watv.org/english/truth/view.html?idx=305""

[47]Korea, The Country in the East, at the Ends of the Earth", http://text.watv.org/"
english/truth/view.html?idx=294

[48]God Will Come From the East", http://text.watv.org/english/truth/"
view.html?idx=295

[49]The Parable of the Fig Tree", http://text.watv.org/english/truth/view.html?idx=308"

[50]The Revival of the Fig Tree", http://text.watv.org/english/truth/view.html?idx=312"

[51]Instinct to Escape Disasters, But Inevitable Reality", http://english.watv.org/who/" truth.html

[52]The Passover of the New Covenant", http://text.watv.org/english/truth/" view.html?idx=228

[53] http://text.watv.org/english/truth/view.html?idx=258

[54]God Promised to Give Us Eternal Life Through the Passover", http://text.watv.org/" english/truth/view.html?idx=230

[55]God Promised to Give Us Eternal Life Through the Passover", http://text.watv.org/" english/truth/view.html?idx=230

[56]Christ Ahnsanghong, Who Restored the Passover of the New Covenant"," http://text.watv.org/english/truth/view.html?idx=233

[57]Prophecy and Its Fulfillment" ["The Feast of the Firstfruits"], http://text.watv.org/" english/truth/view.html?idx=237

[58]Prophecy and Its Fulfillment" ["The Feast of Trumpets"], http://text.watv.org/" english/truth/view.html?idx=211

[59]The Passover of the New Covenant", http://text.watv.org/english/truth/" view.html?idx=228

[60]The Sabbath Day", http://text.watv.org/english/truth/view.html?idx=197"

[61]Other Ceremonies of Sun Worship, Besides Christmas", http://text.watv.org/" english/truth/view.html?idx=350

[62]Baptism", http://text.watv.org/english/truth/view.html?idx=203"

[63]Baptism and the Book of Life", http://text.watv.org/english/truth/" view.html?idx=207

[64]Veil", http://text.watv.org/english/truth/view.html?idx=238"

[65]Age of the Father, and of the Son, and of the Spirit", http://text.watv.org/english/" truth/view.html?idx=298

[66]Witness, Prayer, and Salvation in Each Age", http://text.watv.org/english/truth/" view.html?idx=302

[67]The Savior in the Age of the Son", http://text.watv.org/english/truth/"view.html?idx=300

[68]Witness, Prayer, and Salvation in Each Age", http://text.watv.org/english/truth/"view.html?idx=302

[69]The Savior in the Age of the Spirit", http://text.watv.org/english/truth/"view.html?idx=301

[70]The Truth Always Prevails", http://text.watv.org/english/truth/view.html?idx=290"

[71]The Spirit", http://text.watv.org/english/truth/view.html?idx=244"